AF903782

BOOK CULTURES, MEDIEVAL TO MODERN

Further Information and Publications

www.arc-humanities.org/series/book-series/

PORTABLE MANUSCRIPTS AND THEIR UTILITY IN THE LATE MIDDLE AGES

by

JULIA BRUCH,
KATHARINA M. HOFER,
ULLA KYPTA, and
PAUL SCHWEITZER-MARTIN

ARC HUMANITIES PRESS

British Library Cataloguing in Publication Data
A catalogue record for this book is available from the British Library.

© 2025, Arc Humanities Press, Leeds

The author(s) assert(s) their moral right to be identified as the author(s) of their part of this work.

Permission to use brief excerpts from this work in scholarly and educational works is hereby granted provided that the source is acknowledged. Any use of material in this work that is an exception or limitation covered by Article 5 of the European Union's Copyright Directive (2001/29/EC) or would be determined to be "fair use" under Section 107 of the U.S. Copyright Act September 2010 Page 2 or that satisfies the conditions specified in Section 108 of the U.S. Copyright Act (17 USC §108, as revised by P.L. 94-553) does not require the Publisher's permission.

ISBN (Hardback): 9781802701920
e-ISBN (PDF): 9781802704068
e-ISBN (ePUB): 9781802704051

www.arc-humanities.org

Printed and bound in the UK (by CPIGroup [UK] Ltd), USA (by Bookmasters), and elsewhere using print-on-demand technology.

Publisher (manufacturer) details: Arc Humanities Press, 14 Clifton Moor Business Village, James Nicolson Link, York YO30 4XG, United Kingdom.

EU Authorized Representative details (for GPSR purposes): Amsterdam University Press, Nieuwe Prinsengracht 89, 1018 VR Amsterdam, The Netherlands. www.aup.nl

CONTENTS

LIST OF ILLUSTRATIONS

PREFACE

THIS BOOK ORIGINATED from a session at the International Medieval Congress in Leeds in July 2023. Julia Bruch, Ulla Kypta, and Katharina M. Hofer spoke on different topics concerning "Mobile Manuscripts, Stable Networks: Written Sources as Connecting Elements in the Late Medieval Holy Roman Empire." Paul Schweitzer-Martin functioned as moderator for the session.

We want to thank Anna Henderson from Arc Humanities Press for encouraging us and giving us the opportunity to write this monograph. Thank you to the whole Arc team, especially Tania Colwell, for your support and smoothly walking us through the publication process. Both the cluster "Understanding Written Artefacts" in Hamburg (Universität Hamburg) and the History Department in München (Ludwig-Maximilians-Universität München) generously covered the costs for the editing and publication process which we are very grateful for. Last, we want to thank Johanna Ecker (Köln) for compiling the maps in this book, Kilian Eham (München) for his help with the editing process, and the anonymous peer reviewer for the advice and suggestions.

Julia Bruch, Katharina M. Hofer, Ulla Kypta,
and Paul Schweitzer-Martin
(July 2025)

Introduction

PORTABLE MANUSCRIPTS AND THEIR FUNCTION IN THE LATE MIDDLE AGES

JULIA BRUCH, KATHARINA HOFER, ULLA KYPTA, and PAUL SCHWEITZER-MARTIN

Manuscripts and the Question of Portability

Merchants were and are mobile people. This is maybe even more true for premodern times than for today's businesspeople who can rely on modern means of immediate communication. However, and this will be discussed in this volume, they also used writing in the form of letters, bills of exchange, account books, etc., as well as orality in the form of representatives, messengers, and networks to communicate across distances.[1] Premodern merchants travelled to various places to buy and sell goods, to meet partners, to forge new business relationships, to assess possible venues for trading, to find debtors reluctant to pay back their dues, or to meet their colleagues and discuss future ways of collaboration.[2] Understanding merchants' mobility and their use of portable manuscripts is hence key to comprehending premodern trade.

This volume contributes to the question of merchants' mobility by focusing on the manuscripts that played a crucial role for and in their travels. Since merchants were mobile, the documents they needed for their trade had to be portable: these objects also travelled frequently, as account books accompanying a merchant on his journey, as letters between merchants, or as notes of agreements or contracts that groups of merchants had reached. Merchants operating across vast regions and engaging with an ever-expanding network of business partners were increasingly confronted with the challenges of coordination and control when managing multiple transactions simultaneously. These challenges were partially overcome through

---

1 On the question of literacy, see Hammel-Kiesow, "Schriftlichkeit"; on representatives, see Kypta, *Kooperative Individualisten*.

2 Mobility and interaction with people in different, sometimes distant locations is a characteristic of (long-distance) merchants in the Middle Ages and is understood as part of their identity, see Fouquet, "Kaufleute auf Reisen."

the use of written records. However, by participating in and expanding this culture of writing, merchants also contributed to the very dynamics of complexity that they were trying to control. Portable manuscripts can therefore be categorized into two distinct forms: firstly, they can be transported by the merchant or a representative of the merchant's organization who is responsible for their authorship; secondly, they can be conveyed on behalf of the merchant or a merchant's organization, primarily to substitute for direct face-to-face interaction. Portable manuscripts connected people, tightened control mechanisms, and strengthened communities and (informal) networks.[3] Studying the portability of manuscripts and their utility hence provides us with insight into the organization of economic connections, provides information about communication mechanisms and knowledge transfer, and gives us a deeper understanding of the culture of merchants in premodern times.

The analysis of portable manuscripts in the context of premodern trade brings together three strands of research that have mostly been pursued separately in economic history: the study of material objects, the study of manuscripts as written artifacts, and the study of pragmatic literacy in the sense of the use of writing for practical purposes. We bring these three areas of research together by analyzing the artifacts as artifacts themselves, as carriers of text, and as the texts they contain. We investigate the interdependence of material and textual element as well as the interplay between text, material, and individual. In each instance, the individual and the artifact are inextricably linked by a single defining characteristic: the individual's capacity for mobility and the artifact's inherent portability.

The three chapters following the introduction shed light on merchants' practices by discussing three case studies on manuscripts written by and for merchants from the Holy Roman Empire during the fifteenth and sixteenth centuries. The case studies analyze the function of portability in order to find out more about the workings of trade in premodern society. In sum, this volume brings together cultural and economic history to explore the societal, economical, and cultural background of merchants and their manuscripts. The materiality of artifacts can give insights into the society and cultural context they were produced and used in. Portable manuscripts created, consolidated, and sustained networks of people and communities. The mobility of manuscripts entangled them in their respective society. Studying

3 We use a broad definition of the term "network," which is intended to describe connections between people; for more on the complexity of the term "network," see Hitz, "Network Analysis."

mobility thus connects the material aspects of manuscripts with their social, economic, and cultural context.

Before we dive deeper into premodern merchants' writing cultures, this introduction first sets the scene and describes the basic framework of trade in late medieval Europe and in the Holy Roman Empire in particular, and explores why this is a fruitful period and place to study merchants' manuscripts. We then present the state of the field in the three areas of research relevant for us, namely, material objects in economic history, manuscript studies, and pragmatic literacy. We also outline our analytical approach to analyze the function of the portability of manuscripts and present a short overview of the three case studies.

Setting the Scene

Merchants in the Late Middle Ages

The merchants whose manuscripts are in focus here were active in trade in the late medieval Holy Roman Empire, just like the Hanse merchant Georg Gisze presented in the picture (fig. 0.1) holding a letter in his hand, thereby showing that merchants used to write all the time. In the late Middle Ages, trade continued to flourish in Europe, despite a sharp contraction in economic activities as a whole with the outbreak of the plague in the fourteenth century. Trading networks and connections seem to have been established well enough to continue working even after the population shrank by a quarter or even a third.[4] Economic historians usually distinguish two main trading areas in Europe, the Mediterranean trading circle in the south and the Baltic trade routes in the north of the continent. In the Mediterranean theatre of trade, Italian merchants were the main actors. In particular, merchants from the northern Italian city states such as Florence, Pisa, Venice, and Genoa connected the northern Mediterranean shores with the Arab world south and east of the sea. Italian merchants had outposts at the important Arab trading centres such as Alexandria, Aleppo, and Tunis and thus access to goods that came from the near and far east, such as spices or silk, which they brought to Europe.[5]

In northern Europe, the main connections between the east and the west were serviced by the Hanse merchants, traders from various, mostly German-speaking towns situated in Westphalia and in the coastal areas of

4 For a comprehensive history of the Black Death see Benedictow, *The Black Death*.

5 Remie Constable, *Housing the Stranger in the Mediterranean World*.

Figure 0.1. Hans Holbein the Younger, *Portrait of Georg Gisze* (a Hanse merchant from Danzig, in London), 1532. Oil on oak panel, 96.3 × 85.7 cm. Berlin, Gemäldegalerie, Staatliche Museen zu Berlin. Public Domain.

the North and Baltic Sea.[6] Hanse merchants linked the highly urbanized areas of Flanders with its cloth production centres, northern France and the Rhineland with the much less densely occupied areas to the east, in today's Poland, Russia, and the Baltic. They shipped cloth to the east and timber, ash, amber, and wax to the west. Both theatres of trade met at Bruges, the

6 Hammel-Kiesow, *Die Hanse.*

main trading hub of the late Middle Ages.[7] The Hanse merchants ran one of their important outposts here, and various Italian cities also organized their own houses where the merchants could stay, store their goods, and meet members of their community who could help them if they ran into trouble.

Evidence suggests that merchants from both large trading areas travelled long distances to organize this trade, and that merchants in both regions used pragmatic writing.[8] The written documents that originated in these areas are, to a large extent, transportable, including letters, bills of exchange, guarantees, and letters of recommendation. In addition, especially in the Mediterranean area, merchants encountered cultures whose writing systems were also highly developed, and which used mobile written documents to organize their trade, e.g., merchants' documents found in the Cairo Genizah.[9]

Trade was not only organized by travelling individuals or manuscripts, but also through subsidiaries in foreign cities. Late medieval merchants residing in a foreign city typically formed such groups, often called *nationes* (nations), because it helped them to organize mutual assistance and also to negotiate with the local ruler to grant them certain privileges. In Bruges, Hanse merchants secured important privileges during the thirteenth and fourteenth centuries which guaranteed them, for instance, fixed tariffs and juridical support against debtors reluctant to pay their dues.[10] Similar privileges were granted to the merchants from Genoa, Venice, and various other merchant communities who helped make Bruges the main point of exchange between northern and southern, eastern, and western Europe.

Quite famous among medieval merchants was the Bruges cloth hall: cloth and dyes can be regarded among the main trading goods in European exchange, and the cloth hall in Bruges featured silk, linen, fustian, and wool in various colours of the rainbow, for instance, red made from madder or blue made from woad. Medieval merchants did not specialize in one commodity, however, but traded with various goods in order to mitigate risks. When, for example, a shipload of rice got wet and could not be sold, profits from the sale of salt or timber could counterbalance the losses.[11] Besides,

7 Murray, *Cradle of Capitalism*.

8 Arlinghaus, *Zwischen Notiz und Bilanz*; Lang, *Wirtschaften als kulturelle Praxis*; Hammel-Kiesow, "Schriftlichkeit."

9 Goldberg, *Trade and Institutions in the Medieval Mediterranean*.

10 Jenks, "Transaktionskostentheorie und die mittelalterliche Hanse."

11 Sometimes, nevertheless, everything went wrong at once and the merchants

in comparison with today, supply chains were shaky at best, so merchants could never be completely sure which goods they would find at a certain market or fair, and they were used to keeping their eyes open for bargains and opportunities.

Nevertheless, we can identify some key commodities in premodern trade: firstly, apart from cloth and dyes, various foodstuffs were shipped across the continent. Grain trade, for example, between the different towns in northern Italy could help to alleviate famines, and grain from Prussia was transported by Hanse merchants to the Netherlands to feed the people living in Ghent, Bruges, Antwerp, Bergen op Zoom, and other Flemish and Brabantian towns.[12] Fish formed an important part of the medieval diet because it was allowed to be consumed on feast days and thus herring from the Baltic Sea or stockfish from Norway were exported to the south to provide for the European population.[13] Dishes across Europe were secondly flavoured by salt, for example, from the French salt mines, and spices bought by Italian merchants from Arab merchants who had imported them from the far east. Thirdly, merchants traded raw materials, such as silver from the mines in Tyrol or Bohemia to various minting places across the continent,[14] iron to build tools and weapons,[15] or timber from the forests of Pomerania to the shipbuilding docks in the Netherlands.[16]

This outline of economic structures describes European trade as it existed from the twelfth century onwards. Around that time, a great transformation of trade came to a close. This transformation is usually called the "Commercial Revolution" in economic history, written with capital letters (like the Industrial Revolution) to highlight its importance.[17] Two major changes happened during this revolution: first, the volume of trade surged. Due to a warm climate, the cultivation of crops flourished, and population grew.[18] Peasants produced surpluses they could trade, and they could feed people not working in agriculture, like artisans and merchants.

---

went bankrupt. That happened to Hildebrand Veckinchusen, who will be introduced below; see Hammel, "Veckinchusen, Hildebrand."

12 Link, *Der preußische Getreidehandel im 15. Jahrhundert.*

13 Jahnke, *Das Silber des Meeres*; Holterman, *The Fish Lands.*

14 Zaoral, "Mining."

15 Opll, *Stadt.*

16 Alibhai, "Tale of Two Ports."

17 Lopez, *The Commercial Revolution of the Middle Ages.*

18 Cipolla, *Before the Industrial Revolution.*

Second, the increase in trade volumes induced a transformation of trading practices: merchants no longer travelled with their cargo but cooperated with business partners at different locations. For example, Francesco Datini, a merchant from Tuscany, did not travel himself to Bruges to buy wool from English merchants, but had his agents in Bruges who did the buying.[19] We know more about Francesco Datini than we know about most other medieval merchants, because his letters survived in his house in Prato. The letters were found in 1870, and researchers are still figuring out how to systematize and analyze them,[20] since there are roughly 150,000 in total.[21]

This gives us an impression of how important writing was for medieval merchants, and letters were not the only manuscripts they produced: with partners in different locations, merchants were involved in more than one transaction at a time. Before the Commercial Revolution, when they were travelling with their goods, they completed one act of buying or selling after another, but now they could simultaneously buy wool in Bruges and grain in Genoa, sell diamonds in Paris and spices in Nürnberg because they did not do this themselves, but cooperated with agents in Bruges, Genua, Paris, and Nürnberg. To keep track of all these transactions, merchants wrote account books. To organize the cash flow, they had to write promissory notes, or bills of exchange to transfer money from one place to another. Relations with agents were more and more secured by written contracts and not only by oral agreements, and the same is true for large orders of buying or selling. By and by, the norm was established that important agreements should be written down and ideally kept by an official institution, such as a notary or a city council. Notarial and urban registers that survived, for example, from Marseilles or Antwerp, contain vast amounts of information regarding such contracts.[22]

Hence, during the Commercial Revolution not only did the volume of trade in Europe increase significantly, but because of that, writing and manuscripts became a crucial part of merchants' lives.[23] The importance of

---

19 Origo, *"Im Namen Gottes und des Geschäfts,"* 72.

20 A special focus has been put on his wife Margherita: Cecchi, *Le lettere di Francesco Datini alla moglie Margherita*; Rosati, *Le lettere di Margherita Datini a Francesco di Marco*; James, "A Woman's Work in a Man's World."

21 http://datini.archiviodistato.prato.it, accessed June 30, 2025.

22 Recent studies on the basis of such registers are, among many others, Nicolussi-Köhler, *Marseille, Montpellier und das Mittelmeer*; Kypta, *Kooperative Individualisten*.

23 As Wickham points out, the Italian merchants brought this change to northern Europe, but merchants in other parts of the Mediterranean world, notably in the

writing and cooperating with agents has led to the general impression that merchants were less mobile after the Commercial Revolution. Traditional research usually uses the phrase that merchants became sedentary during this time.[24] However, a closer look at merchants' movements reveals that they still travelled frequently, albeit for other reasons than to sell or buy goods themselves. They sometimes still did that, too, for example when they visited one of the major fairs in Frankfurt am Main, Lyon, and Antwerp, or one of the smaller, but still important fairs in Nördlingen, Wrocław, or Bergen op Zoom. The reason to travel to these fairs, however, was not only to buy or sell goods, but also to watch the market, that is to say, observe which goods were in short or large supply this season, or to examine samples of new products.

Another reason to be mobile was debt collection: since physical currency was always in short supply in the Middle Ages,[25] merchants typically did not pay for their purchases straight away, but rather issued promissory notes or bills of exchange. Merchants thus had to travel to settle the accounts. The payment process did not always go smoothly, and so merchants were quite often involved in various court cases at different places.[26] Sometimes they even relocated to other towns and applied for citizenship there in order to better their chances in a trial, as is known for Peter Karbow, an agent of the Hanse merchant Hildebrand Veckinchusen.[27] Veckinchusen, like Datini, counts among the very few well-known merchants of the Middle Ages because his letters survived.[28] In Veckinchusen's case, his account books are still extant, too,[29] because he went quite spectacularly bust in the 1420s,[30] and his descendants tried to salvage some of his property by entering into court cases with his debtors and associates. To prepare for that, they collected and systematized all his written records. This is quite a typical phenomenon in economic history: we know considerably more about merchants who failed

---

Arab world, practised these new techniques much earlier; Wickham, *The Donkey and the Boat*, 20.

24 See for instance De Roover, "The Commercial Revolution of the 13th Century."

25 Graeber, *Debt*, chap. 10.

26 Höhn, *Kaufleute in Konflikt.*

27 Kluge, "Zwischen Metropole, Fürst und König," 53.

28 Stieda, *Hildebrand Veckinchusen.*

29 Lesnikov, *Die Handelsbücher des hansischen Kaufmanns Veckinchusen*; Lesnikov and Stark, *Die Handelsbücher des Hildebrand Veckinchusen.*

30 Irsigler, "Hildebrand Veckinchusen."

because problems caused the production of texts, and because problems induced economic actors to keep the written documents in case they needed evidence.

A third tier of reasons besides the monitoring of markets and the involvement in debt collection and court cases consists of political activities. Merchants were always on the lookout for political protection because their position was vulnerable: when they or their goods were travelling, they could be robbed and sometimes even held for ransom, and when they stayed in a foreign city, their status was usually lower and more insecure than that of citizens. To better their position, they travelled to princes' courts to obtain letters of safe conduct, and in many important trading cities, as mentioned above, they formed communities to better organize their shared interests. These communities elected elders who represented them in negotiations with the prince or urban authorities, and they thus had to stay for a certain amount of time at the foreign location. Hildebrand Veckinchusen, for example, was a burgher of Lübeck, but spent large chunks of times in Bruges, representing the Hanse merchants at the *kontor* (branch office). All in all, the late Middle Ages were a time when merchants wrote a lot more than before but nevertheless remained mobile and travelled between different places. Their manuscripts, at least the important ones, had thus to be portable so they could be carried.

This was especially true for the fifteenth and sixteenth centuries, the period covered in this book. New trading centres emerged alongside the traditional ones at the Italian, North Sea, and Baltic shores. The transformation of European trade resulted mainly from the endeavours of the Portuguese sailors who had found their way along the coast of Africa to the south and then, to the great astonishments of contemporaries, in 1498 even to Calicut in India.[31] Challenged by the Portuguese advancement, the Spanish king and queen provided Columbus with the means to equip a fleet and pursue his high-risk plan to reach India sailing from Spain to the west. The rest is history: he came upon a continent that was hitherto unknown to the Europeans, which led to the establishment of a sort of exploitative trade with what came to be known as the Caribbean and Southern America. In the long run, this resulted in a shift of the European power centres of commerce from the southeast to the northwest, but during the sixteenth century, new trade routes and the new supply of spices from India, silver, and diamonds

---

31 Epstein, *An Economic and Social History of Later Medieval Europe*, 277–78; Niemann, *Europäische Wirtschaftsgeschichte*, 28.

from America mostly complemented existing trade routes and commodities. Trading activities surged due to new opportunities and the increased supply.

Antwerp can be regarded as the major focal point of this commercial heyday. The city at the mouth of the river Schelde had been a trading centre of medium importance and the place where one could buy English wool for about a century, but when the Portuguese king decided in 1498 that all Portuguese goods from overseas were to be sold in Antwerp, economic activities sharply increased.[32] This created an opportunity especially for merchants from southern Germany who traded with iron and copper from their eastern European mines that was much needed by the Portuguese and the Spanish for their worldwide journeys.[33] The famous southern German trading families like the Fugger and the Welser gained their riches in large part from this trade. Hanse merchants from the Baltic Sea area also saw an increase in their business volumes since they provided, for instance, timber, the essential ingredient for shipbuilding.

In the sixteenth century, merchants hence travelled frequently between the different trading hubs of Europe, from Venice and Genoa to Augsburg and Nürnberg, to Gdansk and Tallinn, to Antwerp and Lisbon. The Commercial Revolution had successfully transformed trading techniques, and the merchants were putting them to full use. In the seventeenth century, things began to change again: most importantly, England and the newly independent Netherlands started to challenge the Portuguese and Spanish in East Asia and America, creating a new form of business venture that turned out to be extremely influential in the history of the modern economy, namely, the East India Companies.[34] These companies were something new because they were backed by state monopolies and because they could act as legal entities, for example, they could own property. Such novel companies were soon established not only for trade with India, but for several world regions, but the principle remained the same and paved the ground for the combination of economic activities and political rule that shaped European colonialism in modern times.

This is a story of later centuries than the ones covered in this book, but it is important in so far as the success of the Dutch and English worldwide endeavours spawned the interest of Dutch and British historians who are

---

32 Van der Wee and Materné, "Antwerp as a World Market"; Limberger, "No Town in the World Provides More Advantages."

33 Harreld, *High Germans in the Low Countries.*

34 Lawson, "The Nature of the Firm and the Peculiarities of the Corporation," 22; Harris, *Going the Distance.*

to this today more active in the field of economic history than German historians. The same is true for Italian economic history. Since Italian merchants played the most influential role in the history of medieval trade, and Dutch and English merchants significantly shaped early modern trade relations between Europe and the world, research has focused mostly on these regions. The fifteenth and sixteenth centuries, the time we are interested in here, can be regarded as the period when the transformation from a Mediterranean-based to an Atlantic-based economy took place. One of the longest-standing debates of economic history discusses the question of whether these transformative processes laid the ground for Europe's "great divergence" from the rest of the world,[35] with Europe (firstly and especially its northwestern parts) experiencing hitherto unknown growth rates of per-capita GDP in the nineteenth and twentieth centuries.[36]

Holy Roman Empire

Other regions than Italy, England, and what is today the Netherlands and Belgium, feature much less prominently in the influential narratives of economic history, and this is especially true for central and eastern Europe. This asymmetry of interest is not only due to the fact that historians prefer to tell success stories, but is also grounded in a lack of research publications in English.[37] Furthermore, what research there is on the German premodern economy typically focuses only on one part of it, on important cities,[38] on the Hanse towns in the North,[39] or on the large trading companies in the South.[40] It is our intention to address this gap, and in particular to underline that there are many and various sources that can be studied to get a clearer image of how trade worked in the late medieval Empire. By bringing

---

35 Pomeranz, *The Great Divergence.*

36 The question of why this happened in Europe, a distorted and poor region of the medieval world, has sparked a huge debate in economic history, see for example Jones, *The European Miracle*; Hoffman, "Why Was It Europeans Who Conquered the World?"; De Pleijt and van Zanden, "Accounting for the 'Little Divergence.'"

37 A notable exception is Scott, *Society and Economy in Germany*; we address this lack in Kypta, Bruch, and Skambraks, *Methods in Premodern Economic History.*

38 Jahnke, *A Companion to Medieval Lübeck*; Tlusty and Häberlein, *A Companion to Late Medieval and Early Modern Augsburg.*

39 Wubs-Mrozewicz and Jenks, *The Hanse in Medieval and Early Modern Europe*; Brand, *The German Hanse in Past & Present Europe.*

40 For instance, Safley, *Family Firms and Merchant Capitalism in Early Modern Europe.*

together case studies on Hanse towns, southern German merchants and a single merchant who does not fit in one of the well-established categories, we would like to point out that merchants in different parts of the Empire, organized in different forms, still shared some common characteristics: they all had to deal with manuscripts, and to make them portable in order to be able to work with them.

The Holy Roman Empire played an important part in the commercial history of premodern Europe for two reasons: first, due to the complicated power structure of this political entity, many towns succeeded in gaining a large degree of autonomy. Some cities, such as Lübeck and Augsburg, achieved the status of "free cities": in theory, their overlord was the emperor, but he was seldom interested in the minutiae of urban politics. Other towns were officially subjugated to a prince, for example Riga to the archbishop of Riga, or Hamburg to the duke of Holstein. However, the city councils managed to extract a number of important rights from their lords during the high and late Middle Ages, among them the right to give themselves their own laws and organize their own jurisdiction. Since merchants counted among the upper classes of these towns and often dominated (or even monopolized) the city council, they could shape the policies of the town to their advantages, which furthered the commercial success of many German towns.

Second, the Holy Roman Empire simply covered a large area of Europe and is thus important to factor in when writing an economic history of the continent. The German lands bordered on the Netherlands and Italy, and its northwestern part was only a short ship journey away from England, so many German merchants engaged in regular trade with these flourishing regions. Furthermore, it can be seen as a kind of borderland between northern and southern, eastern and western Europe. German merchants brought cloth and saffron from the west to the east in exchange for furs and timber; they shipped spices, wine, and other Mediterranean goods from Venice and other Italian trading towns to the North, and herring, wax, and other northern European commodities to the south. Important trade routes connected Antwerp with Lübeck and the Baltic Sea, with Köln, Nürnberg, and then Prague and Wrocław.[41] Goods from Italy, when not being shipped across the sea, around the Iberian Peninsula to Antwerp, crossed over the alps at St. Gotthard or Brenner into German lands and further north via the Rhine or via Augsburg and Nürnberg.

---

41 Harreld, *High Germans in the Low Countries.*

Interestingly, during the sixteenth century trade continued to flourish even when the Empire was rocked by religious upheavals that led to political turmoil. After Martin Luther openly declared his criticism of the papal church, the Holy Roman emperor of the time, Charles V, tried to rein him in, but some of the German princes spotted an opportunity to gain more independence by adopting the new faith—besides probably also believing that Luther's criticism of the pope was justified, and the Christian faith actually needed a renewal. Whatever motivated them exactly, tensions escalated to the point that war broke out in 1546/47. A few years later, Catholic and Protestant princes and the emperor agreed in the Peace of Augsburg to some basic rules of cohabitation, but the peace remained fragile. Nevertheless, merchants continued to travel across the various territories, and they obviously found a way to continue their cooperation even with colleagues who did not share their faith any more: merchants from Catholic Köln worked together with merchants from Protestant Lübeck, as will be studied in more detail in chapter 3, and merchants from Protestant Nürnberg sent their adolescents as apprentices for example to Catholic Milan.[42]

The turn from the Middle Ages to early modern times can not only be characterized by the division of the western Christian church, but also by the invention of the printing press. Handwritten documents are seen as typical for the Middle Ages, whereas the modern age is seen as the age of printing. However, as all our case studies show, merchants in the sixteenth century had not much use for printing. An account book was of course easier to draw up by hand, but even the circular sent to all outposts of an enterprise analyzed in chapter 2 or the minutes of the meetings of Hanse towns, distributed to all towns that had been present, were not printed, but written by hand. The age of the manuscript lasted much longer than the traditional medieval-modern divide suggests. Trading activities were organized by manuscripts, by account books, letters, and reports, and since the merchants were mobile, these manuscripts had to travel as well, in other words, they had to be portable. To study portable manuscripts in the trade of the Holy Roman Empire thus gives us a good entry point to better understand crucial features of this key economy of premodern Europe.

---

42 We know about this because the letters survived that the young sons of Linhart Tucher sent to their father in Nürnberg, among them Daniel Tucher who spent part of his apprenticeship in Milan, see Nürnberg, Stadtarchiv, E29/IV, for instance letter no. 109.

State of the Field in Research

Materiality and Economic History

Subsequent to the seminal publications by Arjun Appadurai in the 1980s, contemporary historical studies have placed a particular emphasis on material objects.[43] Much has been written since this time about the possibilities of the approach for historical science. The contributions of Giorgio Riello and Karin Dannehl have proven to be particularly fruitful in this regard.[44] The most significant and influential definition of "material culture" for German-language research was provided by the ethnologist Hans Peter Hahn, who defined it as "the sum of all objects that are used or hold meaning within a society."[45] This approach interprets the material as a system of signs,[46] with objects serving as a means of communication that follows different rules than linguistic communication. Nevertheless, the ability to convey and preserve linguistic expression through writing facilitates the establishment of a record that can be accessed regardless of physical presence, thereby enabling communication with individuals who are either absent or deceased.[47]

The significance of objects, it must be stressed, does not stem from their materiality, but rather from their use. This means that objects are situational, context-dependent, polyvalent, and embedded in social conventions.[48] The messages conveyed through objects are encoded by senders and, ideally, decoded by recipients. This process only functions if the object is recognized as a sign and both sender and recipient share a common code. The attribution of meaning to objects can occur during their production or at a subsequent stage. Objects are frequently interpreted incidentally and unconsciously, with each viewer deriving their own subjective meaning. This

---

43 Appadurai, *The Social Life of Things*; see also the research overview in Bruch, *Sammeln und auswählen, ordnen und deuten*, chap. 1.4.1; Harvey, *History and Material Culture*; Samida, Eggert, and Hahn, *Handbuch Materielle Kultur*; Hahn, *Materielle Kultur*; Dietrich, Lieb, and Schneidereit, "Introduction."

44 Riello, "Things That Shape History"; Dannehl, "Object Biographies"; Marian Füssel succinctly interprets Giorgio Riello's threefold approach to history and material culture for German historical science as three distinct methodologies; see Füssel, *Die Materialität der Frühen Neuzeit*, 436.

45 Hahn, *Materielle Kultur*, 18.

46 Hahn, *Materielle Kultur*, 115–28.

47 Eggert, "Schrift und Dinge"; Schlögl, "Medien der Macht und des Entscheidens."

48 Eggert. "Kultur und Materielle Kultur," 27–28; Kienlin and Widura, "Dinge als Zeichen"; For a definition of conventions, see Friedrich and Krusenbaum-Verheugen, "Konventionalität und die Literatur der Vormoderne."

meaning may differ from the originally encoded message and can undergo modification over time.[49]

Consequently, the study of objects can be undertaken over an extended period, a methodology referred to as "object biographies."[50] Conversely, objects can be examined in relation to the individuals who have shaped and utilized them. The examination of objects can reveal how individual and group identities are expressed, constructed, and affirmed.[51] In Bruno Latour's influential Actor-Network Theory, objects are assigned their own agency, though they are always examined in interaction with humans.[52]

The research approach has hitherto been utilized in the field of premodern economic history, for instance by examining a specific commodity as an object. Kim Siebenhüner's research focused on jewellery and analyzed international entanglements. Consequently, she is able to analyze not only the commercial exchange of these artifacts but also the attributions of meaning associated with them.[53] In contrast, Katharina Simon-Muscheid's examination focused on the analysis of things within their respective social and economic contexts.[54] Another significant research focus pertains to the examination of artifacts as objects of consumption, a field with the potential to yield results concerning the economic, social, and cultural milieu of the premodern era.[55] The examination of luxury objects as part of pawnbroking systems reveals that such items can also play an important role in less sophisticated economic systems. The examination of pawned objects provides new insights into premodern credit systems.[56] Furthermore, objects are examined as media of economic organization, for example tally sticks as objects of credit.[57]

Research in the field of economic history is currently experiencing a period of significant growth and development, with a notable increase in the number of studies being conducted. The presented works represent a select

---

49 Kienlin and Widura, "Dinge als Zeichen," 33–36.

50 Dannehl, "Object Biographies."

51 Bosch, "Identität und Dinge."

52 Latour, *Reassembling the Social*, 63–86.

53 Siebenhüner, *Die Spur der Juwelen*.

54 Simon-Muscheid, *Die Dinge im Schnittpunkt sozialer Beziehungsnetze*.

55 Schmidt-Funke, *Materielle Kultur und Konsum in der Frühen Neuzeit*.

56 Skambraks, "Tally Sticks as Media of Knowledge."

57 Smail, *Legal Plunder*. On materiality and credit in the Middle Ages, see the special issue Nicolussi-Köhler, Skambraks, and Steinbach, *Die Materialität von Kredit*.

sample of the broader range of issues that are being investigated. From a material perspective, manuscripts are also being evaluated; however, at this stage, they have not yet yielded significant contributions to the field of economic history.

Manuscript Culture Studies

This becomes clear if we take into account the role of the documents that merchants produced or helped produce. Recent economic history as we have seen has followed the trend of material history. In Germany, the material turn has been embraced by scholarship in many ways. One way is to study not only the content of written artifacts but also their material features, since these can reveal a great deal about their purpose, production, and usability.[58] The Collaborative Research Centre 933, "Material Text Cultures" (Sonderforschungsbereich 933 "Materiale Textkulturen"),[59] which was a joint enterprise of Heidelberg University and Hochschule für Jüdische Studien Heidelberg, was one of the first major research centres dedicated to this approach. The centre published its findings in numerous monograph studies and edited volumes dedicated to the field of materiality.[60] The centre's publications had a broad interdisciplinary perspective and covered different regions and periods.[61] The aim of the centre was to examine texts written on different materials from non-typographic cultures. The scholars at the centre studied an extensive array of case studies ranging from the ancient Mediterranean to modern day Bali. However, there was a clear focus on ancient and medieval societies.[62] Key concepts and a handbook of materials relevant to the centre were compiled early on.[63] At the end of the twelve-year funding period key concepts were reassessed and findings of the centre

58 Still fundamental for the study of documents, their appearance, and their use, Clanchy, *From Memory to Written Record*.

59 The centre was funded by the DFG (Deutsche Forschungsgemeinschaft; German Research Foundation) from 2011 to 2023.

60 For the centre's book series see https://www.degruyterbrill.com/serial/mtk-b/html?lang=en#volumes, accessed June 30, 2025.

61 That distinguishes it from previous research on materiality in the Middle Ages; see, for example, Keupp and Schmitz-Esser, *Neue alte Sachlichkeit*.

62 See Brockstieger and Schweitzer-Martin, "Preface." On the establishment and history of the CRC 933: Hilgert and Lieb, "Entstehung und Entwicklung." See for the methods of the CRC: Hilgert, "Textanthropologie"; Hilgert, "Materiale Textkulturen."

63 Meier, Ott, and Sauer, *Materiale Textkulturen*.

were published in a concluding volume both in German and English.[64] The centre emphasized the importance of studying the materiality, the topology, and praxeology of objects likewise.[65]

At roughly the same time, a similar research centre was established at Hamburg University. The Collaborative Research Centre (SFB 950) "Manuscript Cultures in Asia, Africa and Europe" developed into what is called in German research grant terminology a cluster of excellence. The cluster entitled "Understanding Written Artefacts" now forms the largest part of an umbrella organization called "Centre for the Study of Manuscript Cultures" (CSMC) in Hamburg. Similar to the centre in Heidelberg, researchers in Hamburg analyze written artifacts stemming from ancient times until today and from various regions of the world, with strong focal points on Africa and Asia.[66] At the core of the cluster lays the cooperation between the humanities, natural sciences, and computer sciences. Research performed in natural sciences is devoted to developing minimally invasive methods of analyzing a broad variety of written artifacts, that is, all objects carrying handwriting, from the beginning of writing to today's digital age. Computer sciences provide methods to process the various kinds of data gathered in different research projects.

The combination of methods from the humanities and the natural sciences has also been pursued at the Wien-based research institution "Centre of Image and Material Analysis in Cultural Heritage" (CiMA).[67] Established in 2014 as part of the project "Analysis and Conservation of Cultural Property—Modern Imaging and Material Analysis Methods for the Visualization, Documentation and Classification of Historical Written Material (Manuscripts)," the interuniversity institution has set itself the task of analyzing historical objects by using non-invasive chemical methods. Major research areas are: image enhancement and material analysis via non-invasive, non-destructive methods (X-ray fluorescence analysis, Fourier transform infrared spectroscopy, multispectral or hyperspectral imaging and Raman); philological analysis (decipherment); and interpretation of the manuscript data. Although the focus in the first years of its existence was on Greek, Slavic, and Latin

64 Dietrich, Lieb, and Schneidereit, *Theorie und Systematik materialer Textkulturen*; Dietrich, Lieb, and Schneidereit, *Theory and Classification of Material Text Cultures*.

65 Hilgert and Lieb, "Entstehung und Entwicklung," 7.

66 For an introduction see Quenzer, Bondarev, and Sobisch, *Manuscript Cultures*.

67 CIMA: Centre of Image and Material Analysis in Cultural Heritage, https://cima.or.at/, accessed June 30, 2025.

manuscripts, fragments and German manuscripts were also included over time. More recently, the focus has shifted to illuminated manuscripts and documents, the analysis results of which can be found in the newly established database "Multimodal Manuscript Representation," or "M3R" for short.[68]

The University of Salzburg—as well as many other institutions—also contributed to the development of the database, which emerged from the interdisciplinary research project DITAH (Digital Transformation of the Austrian Humanities).[69] The "Institut für Realienkunde des Mittelalters und der Frühen Neuzeit" in Austria, or IMAREAL for short, is associated with the University of Salzburg.[70] Their focus is on understanding materiality. They examine what knowledge about materials is stored in their selection, processing, and symbolization. Things and materials are preserved as material objects, in texts or images. IMAREAL conducts interdisciplinary research and combines different perspectives and methods from archaeology, German studies, history, and art history. Digital technologies and methods are developed and used by the institute to find new approaches for cultural studies research and its communication.[71] Parallel to the scientific approaches, the humanities analysis offers contextual insights and historical localization. The results from the natural sciences support and lend precision to the general findings of humanities analysis. This interdisciplinary approach makes it possible to better understand the complex networks of material procurement and processing in a historical context. The synergetic use of methods from the humanities and natural sciences opens up new perspectives and contributes to a more comprehensive understanding of the cultural and material background of the analyzed manuscripts and documents.

An examination of the findings from these research centres reveals a conspicuous underrepresentation of the economic aspects, merchants' culture, and pragmatic literacy of this research direction. This book aims to address this lacuna in the existing studies.

---

68 Multimodal Manuscript Representation (M3R), https://clariah.at/en/projects/multi-modal-manuscript-representations-m3r/, accessed June 30, 2025.

69 DITAH: Digitale Transformation der Österreichischen Geisteswissenschaften, https://www.ditah.at/, accessed June 30, 2025.

70 IMAREAL: Institut für Realienkunde des Mittelalters und der Frühen Neuzeit, https://www.imareal.sbg.ac.at/, accessed June 30, 2025.

71 Keupp and Schmitz-Esser, "Einführung in die 'Neue alte Sachlichkeit,'" 10.

Pragmatic Literacy

The field of research on the materiality of writing surfaces can now be linked back to research on writing in the Middle Ages, which is also experiencing somewhat of a boom.[72] While the period preceding the modern era can be defined as a genuinely oral culture, this oral culture is increasingly supported by writing during the Middle Ages. One significant question that persists in the field of research is the identification of the actual readers and writers of a particular era, the extent of their involvement with written culture, and the various domains of life in which literacy was a factor.[73] This question remains unresolved, but recent research has demonstrated that literacy was a pivotal element not only within the intellectual milieu of monasteries, universities, and courts but also within the everyday life of urban dwellers, including artisans, merchants, and administrative personnel. In particular, research on pragmatic writing, as advanced by the Collaborative Research Centre 231 "Media, Fields, Forms of Pragmatic Writing in the Middle Ages" (Sonderforschungsbereich "Träger, Felder, Formen pragmatischer Schriftlichkeit im Mittelalter") in Münster in the 1980s and '90s, has led to new insights into the interaction between orality and writing.[74] The findings and publications of this research group had a profound and far-reaching impact on German-language research. Furthermore, our research is situated within the broader field of pragmatic writing studies, in particular in our own monographs on accounting and organizational forms of administrations, monasteries, and traders.[75] Subsequent research by Franz-Josef Arlinghaus has provided an inspiring contribution to the area of merchants in Italy, which summarizes the functionality of merchants' trading activities through writing and shows the important role that text and writing played for larger trading houses.[76] His work is considered groundbreaking in that he also takes into account the materiality of accounting. It is at this juncture that our contribution becomes relevant.

---

72 Bruch, *Sammeln und auswählen, ordnen und deuten.*

73 Wendehorst, "Wer konnte im Mittelalter lesen und schreiben?"

74 Keller, *Pragmatische Schriftlichkeit im Mittelalter*; Meier, Hüpper, and Keller, *Der Codex im Gebrauch*; Keller, Meier, and Scharff, *Schriftlichkeit und Lebenspraxis im Mittelalter.*

75 Schweitzer-Martin, *Kooperation und Innovation im Speyerer Buchdruck*; Kypta, *Die Autonomie der Routine*; Bruch, *Die Zisterze Kaisheim.*

76 Arlingshaus, *Zwischen Notiz und Bilanz.*

The distinguishing characteristic of this research is the focus on manuscripts that are not typically the subject of scholarly attention. The documents under discussion are not of the same nature as the precious, ornate manuscripts with the expensive bindings and clear writing concerning important political topics. These manuscripts, which are often inconspicuous, diminutive in size, ephemeral, often poorly legible, unadorned, and lightly bound, rarely grace exhibitions due to their simplicity and functionality. Our research centres on the efficiency of economic communication in these manuscripts, which are characterized by their unadorned nature, diminutive size, and unpretentiousness.

Approach: The Function of Portability

In this book we shed light on an important aspect of the materiality of pragmatic writing: the respective documents were often portable. As the three chapters will show, portable documents come in a wide range of shapes and sizes, from small letters to thick volumes of trading agreements. In order to paint a colourful picture of the merchants' manuscript culture of the late Middle Ages, all chapters discuss different types of manuscripts, used for different purposes and different stages in the life of manuscripts. In this volume portability implies that an object can easily be transported by a single person without the necessity of tools or aids like a carriage or a pack animal.

Portability, of course, did not emerge as a goal in itself, but rather served a certain aim. The three case studies analyze why the manuscripts were portable, what function they served because of their portability. It is important not to confuse "function" with "efficiency." We do not want to claim that portable manuscripts fulfilled their function efficiently or even in the most efficient way. The idea of efficiency has been very prominent in economic history since Douglass C. North and others established New Institutional Economics as the most prominent approach in economic history from the 1970s onwards.[77] The founding fathers of New Institutional Economics claimed that in the long run, only institutions that were efficient could survive.[78] An institution was deemed efficient if it came with lower transaction cost than its alternatives. For example, a broker lowered search and information costs, a subtype of transaction costs, because he saved merchants the trouble of

---

77 Douglass C. North received a Nobel Prize in economics in 1993. For a concise summary of his theory, see North, *Institutions, Institutional Change and Economic Performance*.

78 See for instance North and Thomas, *The Rise of the Western World*.

trying to find business partners on their own and the goods they wanted to buy. However, brokers also costed fees, so in practice it is often hard to gauge whether a particular institution saved costs or not.

What is more, recent research in institutional theory has pointed out that institutions do and did not only survive because they were efficient, but also because of path dependency or because they serve the interests of the influential groups in society.[79] However, to bury the older idea of institutions always being efficient in the long run does not imply that we should stop altogether analyzing the goals institutions attained, since this tells us something about the society shaped by and shaping these institutions.

Portability can be classed as an information institution:[80] No formal rule prescribed that manuscripts had to be transported from one place to another, rather, merchants followed the custom to carry and send manuscripts. New Institutional Economics encourage us to investigate the function this portability fulfilled. To give an example, the sending of letters between the masters of a trading enterprise and their servants made it possible to supervise the servants. Such supervision could also have been achieved by the masters travelling to the different locations where their servants did business. This would have cost them more time, but would have guaranteed further insights into the servants' trading activities and allowed for the transfer of confidential information that could only be exchanged in private conversation. We do not want to argue, thus, that letters were necessarily more efficient than travelling, since it is hard to estimate whether letters all in all lowered transactions costs (because they made travelling less necessary) or increased them (because letters made supervision harder and thus increased the risk of servants acting not in the interest of their masters). But the fact that merchants relied on letters tells us how they organized their business. Apparently, they regarded the constant exchange of information provided by letters as more important than the closer supervision enabled by personal inspection.

Furthermore, we also have to keep in mind that not every function an institution served had to be intended as such. Analyzing the function of portability only enables us to gain a better picture of premodern trade if we

79 Ogilvie, "'Whatever is, is right'?"

80 For a definition of institutions according to New Institutional Economics, see Greif, "The Fundamental Problem of Exchange," 257: "Economic institutions are defined here as a system of social factors—such as rules, beliefs, norms, and organizations—that guide, enable, and constrain the actions of individuals, thereby generating regularities of behavior."

also include long-term effects of portability, which could not be planned, and were sometimes welcomed by the relevant actors and sometimes not. In our case, portable manuscripts facilitated the formation of social networks, which can be consolidated and retrieved over time and across individuals. Portable manuscripts played a significant role in the dissemination of economic, social, and political information, which was vital for facilitating trade, particularly long-distance trade. The portability of manuscripts provided a foundation for the commercial activities of merchants.

Three Case Studies

The three case studies shed light on the portability of three different kinds of manuscripts written for, by, or in connection with medieval merchants. The chapters cover different phases in the life of manuscripts, from production and writing, over the usage and distribution, to the bonding of people, to the building of formal and informal networks and creating merchants' communities. The first study analyzes a hitherto relatively unknown merchant's book, elucidates social and economic networks, and demonstrates how these networks could be sustained and updated with the assistance of a portable manuscript. Moreover, an emphasis on portability and usability provides a basis for more precise delineation of the genre of merchants' books.

The following two chapters utilize two well-known examples from German-speaking research—the Ravensburger Handelsgesellschaft and the Hanseatic League—to investigate novel findings with the new approach. The organizational structure of these two organizations is not examined directly through legal sources; rather, it is analyzed through the examination of letters and records that were exchanged between distant cities, their representatives, and merchants. The studies address the portability of the manuscripts in order to investigate their function within the organization. The aforementioned analyses demonstrate that portable manuscripts were utilized for the dissemination of information, the establishment of networks, and the exertion of power.

The first case study focuses also on the production process, here of merchants' books, and analyzes how these manuscripts shaped the connections of a merchant while travelling with him. In the dynamic commercial networks of the fifteenth-century Holy Roman Empire, merchants were not only geographically mobile in their business activities but also in their use of portable manuscripts. While studies have frequently concentrated on the movements of traders themselves, relatively little attention has been devoted to the journeys undertaken by their written records. This chapter explores the fascinating realm of portable merchants' books, elucidating their significance as indispensable instruments for recording transactions, sustaining social connections, and navigating economic terrains. By undertaking a detailed examination of Hans Bruckner's trading book from Görlitz, this study demonstrates how these manuscripts functioned as indispensable companions on merchants' travels. In doing so, it sheds light on their role in shaping medieval commerce and society.

Hans Bruckner's fifteenth-century merchant's book provides a compelling insight into the operational aspects of medieval trade. The manuscript is distinguished by a non-linear bookkeeping system and resilient, lightweight, limp binding, which made it an important tool for travelling merchants. This chapter explores the distinctive materiality and functionality of Bruckner's book, emphasizing its role in sustaining social and economic networks in motion. By examining Bruckner's book and contrasting it with other merchants' books from the same period, this study illuminates the diverse and pragmatic character of medieval commercial records and their importance in the daily lives of traders. The diverse and practical bindings of fifteenth-century books owned by merchants provide insight into the functionality and portability of these books. By comparing the various formats and uses of these books, the study reveals how they served multiple roles, from serving as merchants' books to forming part of complex social networks. Through a detailed analysis of Bruckner's book, this chapter highlights the importance of portable manuscripts in medieval trade and calls for further comparative research to deepen our understanding of these vital historical records.

The second case study explores manuscripts that travel from merchant to merchant, namely, business information from one of the most famous southern German trading companies. Not only individual merchants kept books in the late Middle Ages. Networks of merchants and trading companies very much also relied on written documents, that often were also portable. The "Große Ravensburger Handelsgesellschaft" is one such example. It was a major trading company run by three families and their associates from southern Germany between 1380 and 1530. The company's headquarters were in the Swabian city of Ravensburg. Besides this main office the merchants also ran branches and warehouses in many locations in Central and Southern Europe.

One means of communicating was to circulate so called *Rekordanzen* between the different branches with a mix of economic and personal news. These letters were each a few pages long and written by hand. So far only the economic content and not the materiality and mobility of these documents has been studied despite them being the backbone of an impressive economic network. The *Rekordanzen*, for instance, were used to calculate how long messengers travelled between warehouses or what was sold in different locations. By focusing on the portability and materiality of the documents other aspects gain significance. This chapter, for example, shows how the company's success, the associates' knowledge, and personal ties within the company relied on the flow of information through these portable documents. While these findings do not contradict previous research, they certainly provide a different perspective.

The third case study shows how the mobility of manuscripts helped to organize a community of merchants, the Hanse, and how the manuscripts get multiplied in this process. Portability of documents also played an important part in merchants' political organization. In the late medieval Empire, the cooperation between various northern German towns known as Hanse might be the most prominent example. Merchants from cities ranging from Nijmegen to Reval (Tallinn) and from Köln to Gdansk worked together at trading outposts from the thirteenth century onward and spawned the cooperation of their hometowns. From the middle of the fourteenth to the middle of the seventeenth century, representatives of the town councils met every few years at diets to discuss matters of a common economic policy.

This network of towns was not founded on a charter or constitution. To enable cooperation, the towns had to accept the diets as a legitimate governing body, and they did only do that if they felt Hanse cooperation to be a common project that they could participate in creating and shaping. The portability of documents played a crucial role in ensuring that the Hanse towns were included in diets. The chapter shows this by analyzing the documents sent before, during, and after the two Hanse diets of 1418 and 1518. Before the diets, invitations and the agenda of the diet were sent from Lübeck to the other towns and were also circulated and discussed among the cities from the same region. At the diets, town councillors consulted the instructions from their home councils and dispatched reports back home, making sure that the councils were involved in the proceedings. Furthermore, the towns acted as an entity when they dispatched letters written in the name of the diet as one community. After the diet, the minutes (*Rezesse*) were dispatched to every town that had participated at the assembly. The portability of the different exemplars of the *Rezesse* hence ensured that each town participated in creating a kind of shared archive of the proceedings at the diets. This also enabled the town councils to make copies and excerpts of the *Rezesse* and bring them to the next meeting as argumentative aids. All in all, the portability of documents created the network of towns and a sense of community, strengthening the legitimacy of the diets and thus making cooperation work.

In conclusion, the analysis of medieval manuscripts across different contexts demonstrates that portability served different purposes, legal, economic, and political. The movement of manuscripts underscores the interconnectedness of medieval merchants' societies. Across these case studies, the mobility of manuscripts emerges as a key factor in shaping legal, economic, and political systems in medieval Europe, emphasizing the importance of portable documents in fostering networks, sustaining social bonds, and enhancing cooperation. The three chapters share a common focus on portability and usability, as well as a focus on the materiality of manuscripts, their production and use, the interaction between text and material, and between text, material, and the individual. In summary, these chapters collectively highlight the crucial role that the materiality, portability, and usability of manuscripts played in shaping the social, economic, and political networks of medieval Europe. By bringing together economic history and manuscript studies, the chapters offer a comprehensive understanding of how manuscripts not only facilitated trade, governance, and communication, but also connected diverse groups of people—from merchants to city representatives and rulers.

Bibliography

Primary Sources

Le lettere di Francesco Datini alla moglie Margherita. Edited by Elena Cecchi. Prato: Società pratese di storia patria, 1990.

Le lettere di Margherita Datini a Francesco di Marco (1384–1410). Edited by Valeria Rosati. Prato: Cassa di Risparmi e Depositi, 1977.

Secondary Works

Alibhai, Ali Asgar Hussamuddin. "A Tale of Two Port Cities: Al-Mahdiyya, Palermo, and the Timber Trade of the Medieval Mediterranean." *Convivium: Exchanges and Interactions* 10 (2023): 46–67.

Appadurai, Arjun, ed. *The Social Life of Things: Commodities in Cultural Perspective.* Cambridge: Cambridge University Press, 1986.

Arlinghaus, Franz-Josef. *Zwischen Notiz und Bilanz: Zur Eigendynamik des Schriftgebrauchs in der kaufmännischen Buchführung am Beispiel der Datini/ di Berto-Handelsgesellschaft in Avignon (1367–1373).* Gesellschaft, Kultur und Schrift 8. Frankfurt am Main: Lang, 2000.

Benedictow, Ole J. *The Black Death 1346–1353: The Complete History.* Woodbridge: Boydell, 2004.

Bosch, Aida. "Identität und Dinge." In *Handbuch Materielle Kultur: Bedeutung—Konzepte—Disziplinen.* Edited by Stefanie Samida, Manfred K. H. Eggert, and Hans Peter Hahn, 70–77. Stuttgart: Springer, 2014.

Brand, Hanno, ed. *The German Hanse in Past & Present Europe: A Medieval League as a Model for Modern Interregional Cooperation?* Groningen: Castel International, 2007.

Brockstieger, Sylvia and Paul Schweitzer-Martin. "Preface." In *Between Manuscript and Print: Transcultural Perspectives, ca. 1400–1800.* Edited by Sylvia Brockstieger and Paul Schweitzer-Martin, v–viii. Materiale Textkulturen 40. Berlin: De Gruyter, 2023.

Bruch, Julia. *Sammeln und auswählen, ordnen und deuten: Geschichte(n) schreibende Handwerker und ihre Chroniken im 15. und 16. Jahrhundert.* Städteforschung A: Darstellungen. Köln: Böhlau, forthcoming.

——. *Die Zisterze Kaisheim und ihre Tochterklöster: Studien zur Organisation und zum Wirtschaften spätmittelalterlicher Frauenklöster mit einer Edition des "Kaisheimer Rechnungsbuches."* Vita regularis: Ordnungen und Deutungen religiosen Lebens im Mittelalter 5. Berlin: LIT, 2013.

CIMA: Centre of Image and Material Analysis in Cultural Heritage. Accessed June 30, 2025. https://cima.or.at/.

Cipolla, Carlo M. *Before the Industrial Revolution: European Society and Economy, 1000–1700.* London: Methuen, 1976.

Constable, Olivia Remie. *Housing the Stranger in the Mediterranean World: Lodging, Trade, and Travel in Late Antiquity and the Middle Ages.* Cambridge: Cambridge University Press, 2004.

Dannehl, Karin. "Object Biographies: From Production to Consumption." In *History and Material Culture: A Student's Guide to Approaching Alternative Sources.* Edited by Karen Harvey, 123–38. London: Routledge 2009.

Dietrich, Nikolaus, Ludger Lieb, and Nele Schneidereit. "Introduction." In *Theory and Classification of Material Text Cultures: Concluding Volume of the CRC 933*. Edited by Nikolaus Dietrich, Ludger Lieb, and Nele Schneidereit, 1–28. Materiale Textkulturen 46.2. Berlin: De Gruyter, 2024.

Dietrich, Nikolaus, Ludger Lieb, and Nele Schneidereit, eds. *Theorie und Systematik materialer Textkulturen: Abschlussband des SFB 933*. Materiale Textkulturen 46.1. Berlin: De Gruyter, 2023.

——. *Theory and Classification of Material Text Cultures: Concluding Volume of the CRC 933*. Materiale Textkulturen 46.2. Berlin: De Gruyter, 2024.

DITAH: Digitale Transformation der Österreichischen Geisteswissenschaften. Accessed June 30, 2025. https://www.ditah.at/.

Eggert, Manfred K. H. "Kultur und Materielle Kultur." In *Handbuch Materielle Kultur: Bedeutung—Konzepte—Disziplinen*. Edited by Stefanie Samida, Manfred K. H. Eggert, and Hans Peter Hahn, 22–31. Stuttgart: Springer, 2014.

——. "Schrift und Dinge." In *Handbuch Materielle Kultur: Bedeutung—Konzepte—Disziplinen*. Edited by Stefanie Samida, Manfred K. H. Eggert, and Hans Peter Hahn, 47–56. Stuttgart: Springer, 2014.

Epstein, Steven A. *An Economic and Social History of Later Medieval Europe, 1000–1500*. Cambridge: Cambridge University Press, 2009.

Fouquet, Gerhard. "'Kaufleute auf Reisen': Sprachliche Verständigung im Europa des 14. und 15. Jahrhunderts." In *Europa im späten Mittelalter: Politik—Gesellschaft—Kultur*. Edited by Rainer Christoph Schwinges, Christian Hesse, and Peter Moraw, 465–87. Historische Zeitschrift 40. München: Oldenbourg 2006.

Friedrich, Udo and Christiane Krusenbaum-Verheugen. "Konventionalität und die Literatur der Vormoderne: Zur Einführung." In *Kunst und Konventionalität: Dynamiken sozialen Wissens und Handelns in der Literatur des Mittelalters*. Edited by Udo Friedrich, Christiane Krusenbaum-Verheugen, and Monika Schausten, 7–61. Zeitschrift für deutsche Philologie 20. Berlin: De Gruyter 2021.

Füssel, Marian. "Die Materialität der frühen Neuzeit: Neuere Forschungen zur Geschichte der materiellen Kultur." *Zeitschrift für historische Forschung* 42 (2015): 433–63.

Goldberg, Jessica L. *Trade and Institutions in the Medieval Mediterranean: The Geniza Merchants and their Business World*. Cambridge: Cambridge University Press 2012.

Graeber, David. *Debt: The First 5,000 years*. New York: Melville House, 2011.

Greif, Avner. "The Fundamental Problem of Exchange: A Research Agenda in Historical Institutional Analysis." *European Review of Economic History* 4, 251–84. 2000.

Hahn, Hans Peter. *Materielle Kultur: Eine Einführung*. 2nd ed. Berlin: Reimer, 2014.

Hammel, Rolf. "Veckinchusen, Hildebrand." In *Biographisches Lexikon für Schleswig-Holstein und Lübeck*. 9:358–64. Neumünster: Wachholtz, 1991.

Hammel-Kiesow, Rolf. *Die Hanse*, München: Beck, 2021.

——. "Schriftlichkeit und Handelsgesellschaften niederdeutsch-hansischer und oberdeutscher Kaufleute im späten 13. und im 14. Jahrhundert." In *Von Nowgorod bis London: Studien zu Handel, Wirtschaft und Gesellschaft im mittelalterlichen Europa*. Edited by Marie-Luise Heckmann and Jens Röhrkasten, 213–41. Göttingen: Vandenhoeck & Ruprecht, 2008.

Harreld, Donald J. *High Germans in the Low Countries: German Merchants and Commerce in Golden Age Antwerp*. Leiden: Brill, 2004.

Harris, Ron. *Going the Distance: Eurasian Trade and the Rise of the Business Corporation*. Princeton: Princeton University Press, 2020.

Harvey, Karen, ed. *History and Material Culture: A Student's Guide to Approaching Alternative Sources*. London: Routledge, 2009.

Hilgert, Markus. "Materiale Textkulturen: Textbasierte historische Kulturwissenschaften nach dem material culture turn." In *Materialität: Herausforderungen für die Sozial- und Kulturwissenschaften*. Edited by Herbert Kalthoff, Torsten Cress, and Tobias Röhl, 255–68. Paderborn: Fink, 2016.

——. "Textanthropologie: Die Erforschung von Materialität und Präsenz des Geschriebenen als hermeneutische Strategie." *Mitteilungen der deutschen Orient-Gesellschaft zu Berlin* 142 (2010): 87–126.

Hilgert, Markus and Ludger Lieb. "Entstehung und Entwicklung des Heidelberger SFB 933." In *Materiale Textkulturen: Konzepte—Materialien—Praktiken*. Edited by Thomas Meier, Michael R. Ott, and Rebecca Sauer, 7–16. Materiale Textkulturen 1. Berlin: De Gruyter, 2015.

Hitz, Benjamin, "Network Analysis: Social Network Analysis (SNA) and its Derivative, Historical Network Research (HNR)." In *Methods in Premodern Economic History: Case Studies from the Holy Roman Empire, c. 1300–c. 1600*. Edited by Ulla Kypta, Julia Bruch, and Tanja Skambraks, 426–28. Basingstoke: Palgrave, 2019.

Hoffman, Philip T. "Why Was It Europeans Who Conquered the World?" *Journal of Economic History* 72 (2012): 601–33.

Höhn, Philipp. *Kaufleute in Konflikt: Rechtspluralismus, Kredit und Gewalt im spätmittelalterlichen Lübeck*. Frankfurt am Main: Campus, 2021.

Holbach, Rudolf. "'Item das ich Ott Ruland ain kauf hab getroffen': Zu den Handelsgeschäften des Ulmer Kaufmanns im 15. Jahrhundert." In *"Kopet uns werk by tyden": Beiträge zur hansischen und preußischen Geschichte: Walter Stark zum 75. Geburtstag*. Edited by Nils Jörn, Detlef Kattinger, and Horst Wernicke, 81–98. Schwerin: Helms, 1999.

Holterman, Bart. *The Fish Lands: German Trade with Iceland, Shetland and the Faroe Islands in the late 15th and 16th Century*. Berlin: De Gruyter, 2020.

IMAREAL: Institut für Realienkunde des Mittelalters und der Frühen Neuzeit. Accessed June 30, 2025. https://www.imareal.sbg.ac.at/.

Irsigler, Franz. "Hildebrand Veckinchusen: Ein spätmittelalterlicher Hansekaufmann in der Schuldenfalle." Sonderheft, *Zeitschrift für Verbraucher- und Privat-Insolvenzrecht* 8 (2009): 46–50.

Jahnke, Carsten. *Das Silber des Meeres: Fang und Vertrieb von Ostseehering zwischen Norwegen und Italien (12.–16. Jahrhundert)*. Köln: Böhlau 2000.

Jahnke, Carsten, ed. *A Companion to Medieval Lübeck*. Leiden: Brill, 2019.

James, Carolyn. "A Woman's Work in a Man's World: The Letters of Margherita Datini (1384–1410)." In *Francesco di Marco Datini: The Man the Merchant*. Edited by Giampiero Nigro, 53–72. Firenze: Firenze University Press, 2010.

Jenks, Stuart. "Transaktionskostentheorie und die mittelalterliche Hanse." *Hansische Geschichtsblätter* 123 (2005): 31–42.

Jones, Eric. *The European Miracle: Environments, Economies and Geopolitics in the History of Europe and Asia*. Cambridge: Cambridge University Press, 1981.

Keller, Hagen, Christel Meier, and Thomas Scharff, eds. *Schriftlichkeit und Lebenspraxis im Mittelalter: Erfassen, Bewahren, Verändern*. Münstersche Mittelalter-Schriften 76. München: Fink, 1999.

Keller, Hagen, ed. *Pragmatische Schriftlichkeit im Mittelalter: Erscheinungsformen und Entwicklungsstufen*. Münstersche Mittelalter-Schriften 65. München: Fink, 1992.

Keupp, Jan, and Romedio Schmitz-Esser. "Einführung in die 'Neue alte Sachlichkeit': Ein Plädoyer für eine Realienkunde des Mittelalters in kulturhistorischer Perspektive." In *Neue alte Sachlichkeit: Studienbuch Materialität des Mittelalters*. Edited by Jan Keupp and Romedio Schmitz-Esser, 9–46. Ostfildern: Thorbecke, 2015.

Kienlin, Tobias L. and Anne Widura. "Dinge als Zeichen." In *Handbuch Materielle Kultur: Bedeutung—Konzepte—Disziplinen*. Edited by Stefanie Samida, Manfred K. H. Eggert, and Hans Peter Hahn, 31–38. Stuttgart: Springer, 2014.

Kluge, Mathias Franc. "Zwischen Metropole, Fürst und König: Die Venedische Handelsgesellschaft der Kaufleute Veckinchusen und ihr Niedergang." *Hansische Geschichtsblätter* 131 (2013): 33–76.

Kypta, Ulla. *Die Autonomie der Routine: Wie im 12. Jahrhundert das englische Schatzamt entstand*. Historische Semantik 21. Göttingen: Vandenhoeck & Ruprecht, 2014.

——. *Kooperative Individualisten: Gesellschafter, Diener und Bevollmächtigte deutscher Kaufleute im Antwerpen des 15. und frühen 16. Jahrhunderts*. Stuttgart: Steiner, 2025.

Kypta, Ulla, Julia Bruch, and Tanja Skambraks, eds. *Methods in Premodern Economic History: Case Studies from the Holy Roman Empire, c. 1300–c. 1600*. New York: Palgrave, 2019.

Lang, Heinrich. *Wirtschaften als kulturelle Praxis: Die Florentiner Salviati und die Augsburger Welser auf den Märkten in Lyon (1507–1559)*. Vierteljahrschrift für Sozial- und Wirtschaftsgeschichte 248. Stuttgart: Steiner, 2020.

Latour, Bruno. *Reassembling the Social: An Introduction to Actor-Network-Theory*. Oxford: Oxford University Press, 2007.

Lawson, Tony. "The Nature of the Firm and the Peculiarities of the Corporation." *Cambridge Journal of Economics* 39, no. 1 (2015): 1–32.

Lesnikov, Michail P., ed. *Die Handelsbücher des hansischen Kaufmanns Veckinchusen*. Berlin: Akademie, 1973.

Lesnikov, Michail P. and Walter Stark, eds. *Die Handelsbücher des Hildebrand Veckinchusen: Kontobücher und Manuale*. Köln: Böhlau, 2013.

Limberger, Michael. "No Town in the World Provides More Advantages: Economies of Agglomeration and the Golden Age of Antwerp." In *Urban Achievement in Early Modern Europe: Golden Age in Antwerp, Amsterdam and London*. Edited by Patrick O'Brien, Derek Keene, Marjolein t'Hart, and Herman van der Wee, 39–62. Cambridge: Cambridge University Press, 2001.

Link, Christina. *Der preußische Getreidehandel im 15. Jahrhundert: Eine Studie zur nordeuropäischen Wirtschaftsgeschichte*. Köln: Böhlau, 2014.

Lopez, Robert S., *The Commercial Revolution of the Middle Ages: 950–1350*. Cambridge: Cambridge University Press, 1995.

Meier, Christel, Dagmar Hüpper, and Hagen Keller, eds. *Der Codex im Gebrauch*. Münstersche Mittelalter-Schriften 70. München: Fink, 1996.

Meier, Thomas, Michael R. Ott, and Rebecca Sauer, eds. *Materiale Textkulturen: Konzepte—Materialien—Praktiken*. Materiale Textkulturen 1. Berlin: De Gruyter, 2015.

Multimodal Manuscript Representation (M3R). Accessed June 30, 2025. https://clariah.at/en/projects/multi-modal-manuscript-representations-m3r/.

Murray, James M. *Bruges: Cradle of Capitalism, 1280–1390*. Cambridge: Cambridge University Press, 2005.

Nicolussi-Köhler, Stephan. *Marseille, Montpellier und das Mittelmeer: Die Entstehung des südfranzösischen Fernhandels im 12. und 13. Jahrhundert.* Heidelberg: Heidelberg University Publishing, 2021.

Nicolussi-Köhler, Stephan, Tanja Skambraks, and Sebastian Steinbach, eds. *Die Materialität von Kredit: Sachüberlieferungen mittelalterlicher Schuld- und Kreditbeziehungen.* Special issue, *Das Mittelalter: Perspektiven mediävistischer Forschung: Zeitschrift des Mediävistenverbandes* 27, no. 2 (2022).

Niemann, Hans-Werner. *Europäische Wirtschaftsgeschichte: Vom Mittelalter bis heute.* Darmstadt: WBG, 2009.

North, Douglass C. *Institutions: Institutional Change and Economic Performance.* Cambridge: Cambridge University Press, 1990.

North, Douglass C., and Robert P. Thomas. *The Rise of the Western World: A New Economic History.* Cambridge: Cambridge University Press, 1973.

Ogilvie, Sheilagh. "'Whatever is, is right'? Economic Institutions in Pre-Industrial Europe." *The Economic History Review* 60, no. 4 (2007): 649–84.

Opll, Ferdinand, ed. *Stadt und Eisen.* Linz: Österreichischer Arbeitskreis für Stadtgeschichtsforschung, 1992.

Origo, Iris. *Im Namen Gottes und des Geschäfts: Lebensbild eines toskanischen Kaufmanns der Frührenaissance; Francesco di Marco Datini 1335–1410.* Translated by Uta-Elisabeth Trott. München: Wagenbach, 1985.

Pleijt, Alexandra M. de and Jan Luiten Van Zanden. "Accounting for the 'Little Divergence': What Drove Economic Growth in Pre-Industrial Europe, 1300–1800?" In *European Review of Economic History* 20 (2016): 387–409.

Pomeranz, Kenneth. *The Great Divergence: China, Europe, and the Making of the Modern World Economy.* Princeton: Princeton University Press, 2000.

Quenzer, Jörg B., Dmitry Bondarev, and Jan-Ulrich Sobisch, eds. *Manuscript Cultures: Mapping the Field.* Studies in Manuscript Cultures 1. Berlin: De Gruyter, 2014.

Riello, Giorgio. "Things That Shape History: Material Culture and Historical Narratives." In *History and Material Culture: A Student's Guide to Approaching Alternative Sources.* Edited by Karen Harvey, 24–46. London: Routledge, 2009.

Roover, Raymond de. "The Commercial Revolution of the 13th Century." In *Enterprise and Secular Change: Readings in Economic History.* Edited by Frederic C. Lane and Jelle C. Riemersma, 80–85. London: Allen and Unwin, 1953.

Safley, Tom. *Family Firms and Merchant Capitalism in Early Modern Europe: The Business, Bankruptcy and Resilience of the Höchstetters of Augsburg.* London: Routledge 2019.

Samida, Stefanie, Manfred K. H. Eggert, and Hans Peter Hahn, eds. *Handbuch Materielle Kultur: Bedeutung—Konzepte—Disziplinen.* Stuttgart: Springer, 2014.

Schlögl, Rudolf. "Medien der Macht und des Entscheidens: Schrift und Druck im politischen Raum der europäischen Vormoderne (14.–17. Jahrhundert); Eine Einleitung." In *Medien der Macht und des Entscheidens: Schrift und Druck im politischen Raum der europäischen Vormoderne (14.–17. Jahrhundert).* Edited by Rudolf Schlögl and Jan Marco Sawilla, 7–32. Hannover: Wehrhahn, 2014.

Schmidt-Funke, Julia A., ed. *Materielle Kultur und Konsum in der Frühen Neuzeit.* Ding, Materialität, Geschichte 1. Köln: Böhlau 2017.

Schweitzer-Martin, Paul. *Kooperation und Innovation im Speyerer Buchdruck des ausgehenden Mittelalters.* Materiale Textkulturen 37. Berlin: De Gruyter, 2022.

Scott, Tom. *Society and Economy in Germany, 1300–1600.* New York: Palgrave, 2002.

Siebenhüner, Kim. *Die Spur der Juwelen: Materielle Kultur und transkontinentale Verbindungen zwischen Indien und Europa in der Frühen Neuzeit*. Ding, Materialität, Geschichte 3. Köln: Böhlau, 2018.

Simon-Muscheid, Katharina, *Die Dinge im Schnittpunkt sozialer Beziehungsnetze: Reden und Objekte im Alltag (Oberrhein, 14.–16. Jahrhundert)*. Veröffentlichungen des Max-Planck-Instituts für Geschichte 193. Göttingen: Vandenhoeck & Ruprecht, 2004.

Skambraks, Tanja. "Tally Sticks as Media of Knowledge in the Contexts of Medieval Economic and Administrative History." In *L'economia della conoscenza: Innovazione, produttività e crescita economica nei secoli XIII–XVIII*. Edited by Giampiero Nigro, 137–58. Firenze: Firenze University Press, 2023.

Smail, Daniel Lord, *Legal Plunder: Households and Debt Collection in Late Medieval Europe*, Cambridge: Harvard University Press, 2016.

Tlusty, B. Ann, and Mark Häberlein, eds. *A Companion to Late Medieval and Early Modern Augsburg*. Leiden: Brill, 2020.

Veckinchusen, Hildebrand. *Briefwechsel eines deutschen Kaufmanns im 15. Jahrhundert*. Edited and introduced by Wilhelm Stieda. Leipzig: Hirzel, 1921.

Wee, Herman van der, and Jan Materné. "Antwerp as a World Market in the Sixteenth and Seventeenth Centuries." In *Antwerp, Story of a Metropolis: 16th–17th century*. Edited by Jan van der Stock, 19–31. Gent: University of Washington Press, 1993.

Wendehorst, Alfred. "Wer konnte im Mittelalter lesen und schreiben?" In *Schulen und Studium im sozialen Wandel des hohen und späten Mittelalters*. Edited by Johannes Fried, 9–33. Sigmaringen: Thorbecke, 1986.

Wickham, Chris. *The Donkey and the Boat: Reinterpreting the Mediterranean Economy, 950–1180*. Oxford: Oxford University Press, 2023.

Wubs-Mrozewicz, Justyna, and Stuart Jenks, eds. *The Hanse in Medieval and Early Modern Europe*. Leiden: Brill, 2012.

Zoaral, Roman, "Mining, Coinage, and Metal Export in the Thirteenth Century: The Czech Lands and Italy in Comparative Perspective." In *The Medieval Networks in East Central Europe: Commerce, Contacts, Communication*. Edited by Balázs Nagy, Felicitas Schmieder, and András Vadas, 211–26. London: Routledge, 2019.

Chapter 1

PORTABLE MERCHANTS' BOOKS AND THEIR INFLUENCE ON SOCIAL AND ECONOMIC NETWORKS

JULIA BRUCH

THE MOBILITY OF merchants cannot be questioned for the fifteenth century in the Holy Roman Empire; on the contrary, it is emphasized in recent studies.[1] The owners of small and medium-sized stores, in particular, travelled to buy and sell their goods at large and small fairs in villages and towns in the surrounding area, as well as in major cities further afield. As we may see, they took advantage of recurring stays to establish and deepen business contacts. Even though the mobility of traders has already been studied, the mobility of their manuscripts has been neglected, and it is precisely this aspect that will be the focus of this chapter.

The aim is to show that portable merchants' books existed in the fifteenth century and they served as memory aids, stores of social information, and can be read as an image of socio-economic networks. It will be shown that economic contacts were started, consolidated, and expanded with the help of portable manuscripts. Investigations into the content and materiality of the manuscripts can reveal information about the functionality of the manuscripts in an economic and social network and provide a deeper understanding of how traders used writing to conduct their day-to-day business. For my study I propose a combined approach, comprising a critical content analysis and a codicological analysis. I understand manuscripts as an expression of a specific written culture, within which merchants played a role.[2] This study examines the conventionalized practices of bookkeeping on the one hand and the performative practices of the formation of social and economic networks on the other. Additionally, a typification of merchants' books is undertaken.[3]

1 Mähnert and Selzer, *Vertraute Ferne*.

2 See the introduction to this volume.

3 Kypta, "Classification/Types," 401–3.

Using the example of the merchant's book by Hans Bruckner († 1505), this chapter demonstrates that travelling merchants carried manuscripts with them on their journeys for special purposes. I will proceed as follows: first, I present the example manuscript. This will include a historical contextualization of the scribe and a codicological description of the manuscript. I will also give a summary of the content. I will then show that portable manuscripts played a crucial role in bookkeeping and in the management of one's own business.

In the second part of the chapter, I will especially look at the genre of the source and ask what kind of commercial writing is portable. It will be shown that the material composition alone can tell us today whether the book was portable or not. The books were functionally designed to meet the needs of travel. In an extended focus it is shown which other books were carried around in an administrative context to work out more general functions of portable books. Comparison with other, non-portable, merchants' books will be used to work out the function of portable manuscripts.

The Merchant's Book of Hans Bruckner

The Life of Hans Bruckner

This chapter is based on the merchant's book by Hans (Johannes) Bruckner from Görlitz. It is probable that Hans was born in Görlitz, although this cannot be confirmed. The family's property history provides evidence that the family resided in this town. Hans's father's sister, his aunt Agneta Prausinne, a baker, was the proprietor of a house in Görlitz.[4] E. Schulze postulates the possibility of a Nickel Bruckner as his father, whose name is mentioned in the city's *Liber actorum*.[5] An examination of Hans Bruckner's merchant's book reveals that he did not establish his own business enterprise at the outset of his career. Instead, he commenced his professional activities as an employee of other businesses.[6] He was employed by Heinrich Rummel in Nürnberg, who was himself a business partner, publisher, or maybe patron of Johannes Sensenschmidt's[7] print shop, and by the printer Heinrich Eggstein

4 Schulze, "Ein Krämerbuch," 182; Bruckner, *Krämerbuch*, fols. 25r and 26r.

5 Schulze, "Ein Krämerbuch," 182; Görlitz, Stadtarchiv, *Liber actorum 1478–1483*, fol. 19v. Schulze's work provides the first content-based summary of the Krämerbuch, which is of great assistance in accessing the unpublished source.

6 Text passages also collected at Schulze, "Ein Krämerbuch," 182–83.

7 Grimm, "Die Buchführer des deutschen Kulturbereichs," 1194; for further

in Strasbourg.[8] It is probable that Bruckner was employed as a professional book seller (*Buchführer*).[9]

In 1476, Hans Bruckner leased a vault in Görlitz. Prior to June 16, 1478, he married Ursula, daughter of Heintz Schmid and sister of Michel Schmid. Ursula had her brother pay her the inheritance.[10] In 1479, Hans Bruckner purchased a store, known as a *cromen*, which had been established by the Görlitz town council. This purchase was also documented in his book.[11] It is possible that he obtained citizenship in Görlitz in 1481.[12] He acquired a property in 1495 for 415 marks, which was fully repaid in 1496.[13] Schulze postulates that Hans Bruckner relinquished the proprietorship of his enterprise from 1496 onwards, although his merchant's book concludes at this juncture.[14] In 1501, he was appointed to the council, a position he retained until 1503/4. In 1505, Hans Bruckner died without leaving any descendants.[15]

---

information on Sensenschmidt, his business contacts, and his workshop, see Schweitzer-Martin, "Material und Format liturgischer Inkunabeldrucke," 301–2; Schweitzer-Martin, *Kooperation und Innovation im Speyerer*, 190–95.

8 Bruckner, *Krämerbuch*, fols. 49r and 30v; see Schulze, "Ein Krämerbuch aus dem Ende des 15. Jahrhunderts," 182–83; for Heinrich Eggestein and his business in Strasbourg, see Grimm, "Die Buchführer des deutschen Kulturbereichs," 1421–22.

9 The Buchführer distributed books produced by a printer in places other than the place of printing; see Grimm, "Die Buchführer des deutschen Kulturbereichs," 1193–94; in any case, Grimm categorizes Bruckner as a Buchführer, Grimm, "Die Buchführer des deutschen Kulturbereichs," 1708.

10 Bruckner, *Krämerbuch*, fol. 89v; Schulze, "Ein Krämerbuch aus dem Ende des 15. Jahrhunderts," 182.

11 Bruckner, *Krämerbuch*, fol. 60r–v; Görlitz, Stadtarchiv, *Liber actorum 1478–1483*, fols. 72r, 108v; see Schulze, "Ein Krämerbuch aus dem Ende des 15. Jahrhunderts," 182, a reconstruction of the location at Schulze, "Ein Krämerbuch aus dem Ende des 15. Jahrhunderts," 183–84. Hans Bruckner was listed as the second merchant (out of nine) in the 1480s and '90s. Schulze assumes that, due to his range of goods, he was one of the spice and silk merchants in Görlitz who owned fixed cromen alongside the lace and Pudritzkrämer (small merchants). There were a total of eighteen cromen built by the council (Schulze, "Ein Krämerbuch aus dem Ende des 15. Jahrhunderts," 188).

12 If he matches the Hans Bruckner mentioned in the *liber censuum* of the city: "dedit 1 buchsen" (Schulze, "Ein Krämerbuch aus dem Ende des 15. Jahrhunderts," 182).

13 Bruckner, *Krämerbuch*, fol. 70r–v.

14 Schulze, "Ein Krämerbuch aus dem Ende des 15. Jahrhunderts," 184.

15 Schulze, "Ein Krämerbuch aus dem Ende des 15. Jahrhunderts," 184; Schulze edited the will: Schulze, "Ein Krämerbuch aus dem Ende des 15. Jahrhunderts," 185.

Figure 1.1. Bruckner, Krämerbuch, binding. Görlitz, Ratsarchiv/Stadtarchiv, *Varia 70*. Used with permission.

The Materiality of Bruckner's Merchant's Book

Hans Bruckner's merchant's book covers the years 1476 to 1496 and was kept continuously during these years, although the number of entries decreases significantly from 1488 onwards.[16] No entries can be found for the years 1490, 1491, and 1493.[17] The external appearance and composition of the book are significant factors in subsequent categorization: the parchment binding measures 165 mm × 225 mm, with a thickness of 25 mm. The book contains 92 sheets of paper in quarto format. The original binding, which is heavily worn and soiled, had been formerly reinforced with three thick leather

16 Not yet sufficiently analyzed, mentioned in works on the book trade: Mäkeler, *Das Rechnungsbuch des Speyerer Druckherrn Peter Drach d. M.*, 9: here as a "trade book." See also the other known merchants' books for the fifteenth and sixteenth century there (Mäkeler, *Das Rechnungsbuch des Speyerer Druckherrn Peter Drach d. M.*, 8–10) and in Steinbrink, *Ulrich Meltinger*, 18–20.

17 Görlitz, Ratsarchiv/Stadtarchiv, *Varia 70*. See also the manuscript descriptions in Schulze, "Ein Krämerbuch aus dem Ende des 15. Jahrhunderts," 181–82; Jecht, *Quellen zur Geschichte der Stadt Görlitz bis 1600*, 171.

straps, which have been attached to the binding with thin leather straps with cross-stitching (see fig. 1.1).

The thicker leather straps are decorated with punched stars. The stitches go right through the binding. All three leather straps exhibit some degree of damage. The middle strap, which also served as a clasp for the parchment binding, is particularly incomplete.[18] The manuscript description from the nineteenth century indicates that a buckle was attached to this ribbon.[19] The overall weight of the manuscript is relatively light, as the book cover has not been strengthened with wood or cardboard. The paper is of a substantial and uniform quality, and the binding is even.[20] Bruckner's merchant's book contains fragments of other documents. On the interior of the front cover, there is evidence of the removal of a label and the application of an archive stamp. The first few pages of the manuscript have been torn out. The sheets bearing the identical watermark[21] are composed of five distinct quires.[22]

Some of the early pages of the manuscript feature an alphabet on the outer margin with each letter identified by a marker (see fig. 1.2).[23] The codex is divided into sections, with each section containing either an alphabetical index or, in the case of the sections that do not, a numbering system based on Roman numerals at the top of the page.[24] The pen and ink used for the letters and numbers do not correspond to the pen and ink of the main

18 There is a label with the signature Varia 70 on the spine between the upper and centre bands. The label originally extended to the front and back covers. The parchment is visibly lighter in colour there, but these parts of the label are missing. There was also a label between the lower and centre band, which is missing completely. The number 70 was written on the lighter-coloured area between the upper and middle leather bands on the front cover. A number was also written between the centre and lower leather band, which is difficult to read today (possibly also 70).

19 Schulze, "Ein Krämerbuch aus dem Ende des 15. Jahrhunderts," 181.

20 The paper has the following sizes: 220 × 154–155 mm (fols. 2, 42, 57, 68).

21 Description according to Piccard: Triple hill, free, additional inscription, two-contour pole, cross, simple Latin cross, without additional inscription, straight crossbar, simple base line.

22 Scheme according to Anton Chroust; the number of existing sheets is shown in superscript, the current foliation in subscript: $(3\text{-}X-1)^{17}{}_{16}+2xX^{57}{}_{56}+(X-2)^{75}{}_{74}+(X-2)^{92}{}_{91}$.

23 Bruckner, *Krämerbuch*, fols. 1–19. The letters A and B have been excised from the document, and the page containing the letter G is damaged. Additionally, the pages bearing the letters Q and U are either absent or severely damaged. The letters J, V, and W were not included in the original text.

24 Bruckner, *Krämerbuch*, fols. 20–87.

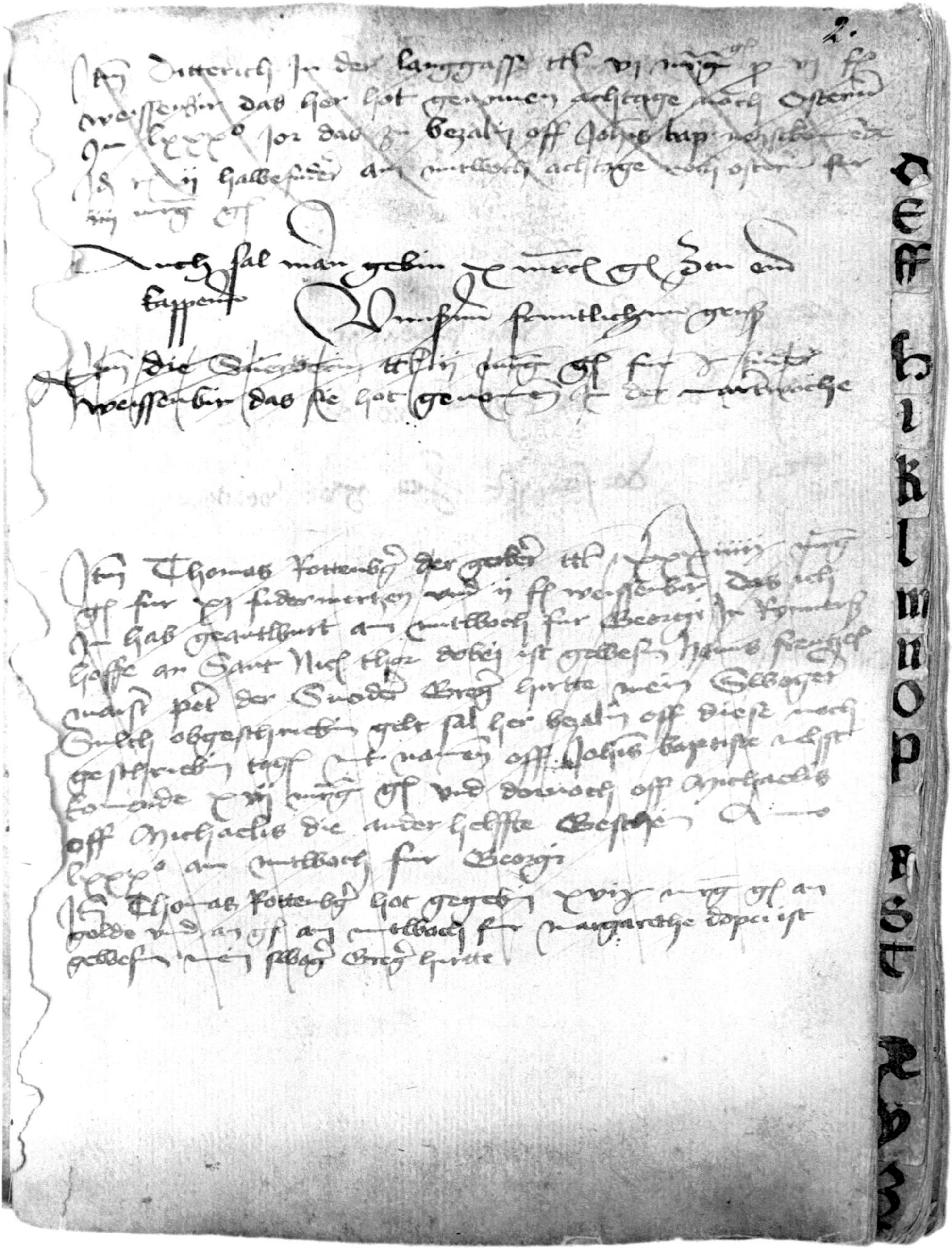

Figure 1.2. Bruckner, Krämerbuch. Görlitz, Ratsarchiv/Stadtarchiv, *Varia 70*, fol. 2r. Used with permission.

text. It is reasonable to posit that the manuscript was structured in this way prior to its utilization as a merchant's book.[25] In addition to the aforementioned planned structure, the manuscript does not exhibit a uniform layout.[26] Schulze has already observed that neither a chronological nor an alphabetical order can be discerned.[27]

Two distinct scribes are evident in the entries, with one being identified as Hans Bruckner and the other remaining anonymous.[28] The entries by the principal scribe (i.e., Bruckner) are perfunctory but still legible, indicating a certain degree of expertise. A significant proportion of the entries have been crossed out (see fig. 1.2). The second hand has left a considerably smaller number of entries, and the writing is more irregular. The entries are primarily concerned with the beer and grain trade. The presence of a date allows for the assumption that some of the later entries were made in the year 1519.[29] Hans Bruckner employs a variety of entry types. The almost three hundred entries can be classified as a mixture of Latin and vernacular. German is the predominant language for goods, while Latin is used for commercial terms such as *Item*, *tenetur*, *dedi*, and *Anno*.

The entries are introduced with the designation *Item*, line breaks or free lines indicate the end of the entries (see fig. 1.2). The term *idem* is employed for internal structuring in longer entries. The entries initially function without an entry record (*Eingangsprotokoll*). An *item* marks the beginning and

25 The codex also features modern numbering with Indo-Arabic numerals: After foliation of the leaves, fol. 17 has been lost, fol. 62 has been cut off, fols. 1, 5, and 13 are torn with loss of text. Before the foliation, two leaves are lost at the beginning of the first quire (remains present), at the end of the first quire (between 16 and 17 after the foliation), between 71 and 72 two leaves are lost before the foliation, as well as between 88 and 89 (remains recognizable) at the end of the last quire one leaf has been lost, when is unknown.

26 On the recto pages the inner margin varies between 14 and 17 mm (fols. 37, 57, 73); on the verso pages the outer margin varies between 10 and 14 mm (33, 46). From fol. 64 onwards, the layout generally becomes more generous and irregular. The modern foliation is used here.

27 Schulze, "Ein Krämerbuch aus dem Ende des 15. Jahrhunderts," 181–82.

28 The main writer occasionally refers to himself in the entries, for example: *Jch Hanns Bruckner bin schuldig* (I Hans Bruckner owe; Bruckner, *Krämerbuch*, fol. 11br); *Jt(e)m Jch Hanns Bruckn(er) zu Gorlitz hab gekaufft diese nachgeschrieben war zu Laptzig* (Item, I Hans Bruckner from Görlitz have bought the following goods in Leipzig, fol. 41r); "Jch Hanns Bruck(n)er habe ~~ab~~gekaufft eine(n) cromen von den ersam(en) vnd weisen h(er)ren" (I Hans Bruckner have bought a shop from the honourable and wise men, fol. 57r).

29 See also Schulze, "Ein Krämerbuch aus dem Ende des 15. Jahrhunderts," 181.

is immediately followed by the name and the word *tenetur* (usually as an abbreviation), and then the goods, possibly (but not always) an indication of the debt amount (with the introductory word *vor*), followed at the end by the day and year of the transaction. In some instances, the amount of the debt was indicated prior to the goods, with the latter item also preceded by a *vor*.[30]

The Function of Bruckner's Merchant's Book

In essence, Bruckner's merchant's book can be characterized as a compendium of debts.[31] The text encompasses both creditor-debtor and debtor-creditor relationships. Bruckner is both a creditor and a debtor. In this context, it is possible to place occasional invoices that Bruckner made for longer-term credit transactions.[32] Furthermore, it is uncommon for payments to be recorded without a credit link.[33] Several entries that refer to cash payments were made via intermediaries.[34] Additionally, the merchant's book contains a notarized account of a robbery (69r) and a house purchase (69v–71r). The receipts for payments made by the brother-in-law Michel Schmidt, due to an inheritance, can also be found (89v–90r), as well as the receipts for payments to the city of Görlitz regarding the aforenoted store (60r–61r). An obituary for Seyffrid Geßwin has also been inscribed in the book (91v).

The written documentation of credit relationships creates a certain additional obligation, which is a subject of investigation in the field of trust and mistrust.[35] It is not possible to ascertain whether Bruckner engaged in other written or tangible forms of debt fixing in his business dealings—like tally sticks or chirographs. However, it is generally understood that such practices were common.[36] The act of writing in the debt register is understood

---

30 E.g., Bruckner, *Krämerbuch*, fols. 6v, 9r, 10r.

31 Furthermore, Arlinghaus observed that account books can serve as debtor-creditor registers, based on their primary content (Arlinghaus, *Zwischen Notiz und Bilanz*, 349–52). The merchant's book of the Reval merchant Bernd Pal is referenced in the archive and in research as a debt book; for further information on Pal, see Jahnke, "Bernd Pal, ein Kaufmann des 15. Jahrhunderts," 158–76.

32 Bruckner, *Krämerbuch*, fols. 11av–11br, 21v, 24v, 33v, 37r, 45v, 47r, 72r, 74r, 78v, 89r.

33 Bruckner, *Krämerbuch*, fols. 8r, 13v, 15v–16r, 33r.

34 Bruckner, *Krämerbuch*, fols. 8r, 12v, 13v, 16v, 33r.

35 On trust as the basis of economic behaviour, see the articles in: Hirschbiegel, Welser, and Westermann, *Ökonomisch bestimmtes Handeln in der Vormoderne*.

36 Skambraks, "Tally Sticks as Media of Knowledge," 137–58; Skambraks, "Die moralische Ökonomie des steirischen Kaufmanns Clemens Körbler."

here as a performative practice that not only makes the transaction memorable (like tally sticks or chirographs), but also becomes tangible as a materialization of the social and economic connection between the actors. The trading partners are inscribed in Bruckner's network in a literal sense. This also enables Bruckner to call up connections at any time. Other methods of maintaining debt relationships become irrelevant once the debt has been settled. Nevertheless, Bruckner's merchant's book permits the continued existence of these former debt relationships as social and economic relationships. It is therefore not surprising that these relationships can be reactivated. This is exemplified by the entries on Magister Peter Scheit, an altarist (chaplain) in Görlitz (23v–24v). In 1476, Peter Scheit made a substantial purchase from Hans Bruckner, which he subsequently repaid by 1477. Thereafter, he made another purchase from Hans Bruckner in 1479. Bruckner was able to combine those two purchases in his book, he notes the second one properly in a subsequent entry. This is followed by an accounting from 1482. Further examples of long-term business relationships include that of Jakobus Sluckenwerder, an altarist in Wrocław, who purchased from Bruckner between 1477 and 1481. Another such relationship is that of Caspar Besser in Leipzig, from whom Bruckner purchased in 1484, 1485, 1488, and 1492.[37] The credit relationships with individual players were not always managed with the same degree of care as in the three cases previously mentioned. Rather, longer-term debt relationships can be distributed across the entire merchant's book, as exemplified by the relationships with Hans Fackeler,[38] Hans Rogewitz,[39] and Hans Brewer, *der Weinschenk*.[40]

Noteworthy is his brother-in-law, Georg Hirte, with whom he repeatedly settled accounts. In addition to the aforementioned altarists, other purchasers of his stock were to be found in Görlitz, including other merchants, citizens, and residents. His trading network extended beyond Görlitz, however, and he maintained regular trading contacts with merchants in Leipzig and Wrocław in particular. There Hans Bruckner participated in the larger trade fairs, the New Year's Fair in Leipzig and the St. Elisabeth's Market in Wrocław. His contacts with Dresden, Bautzen, and Legnica, on the other hand, were less frequent, but there is evidence for trips to these cities

37 Bruckner, *Krämerbuch*, fol. 39r–v; fols. 58r, 66r–67r.

38 1480 (Bruckner, *Krämerbuch*, fols. 42r–43v), 1482–1483 (50v), 1483 (53v), 1486 (64r).

39 1480 (Bruckner, *Krämerbuch*, fols. 15r), 1485 (13v).

40 1476 (Bruckner, *Krämerbuch*, fol. 21r), 1477 (80r), 1478 (19r, 33r, 33v).

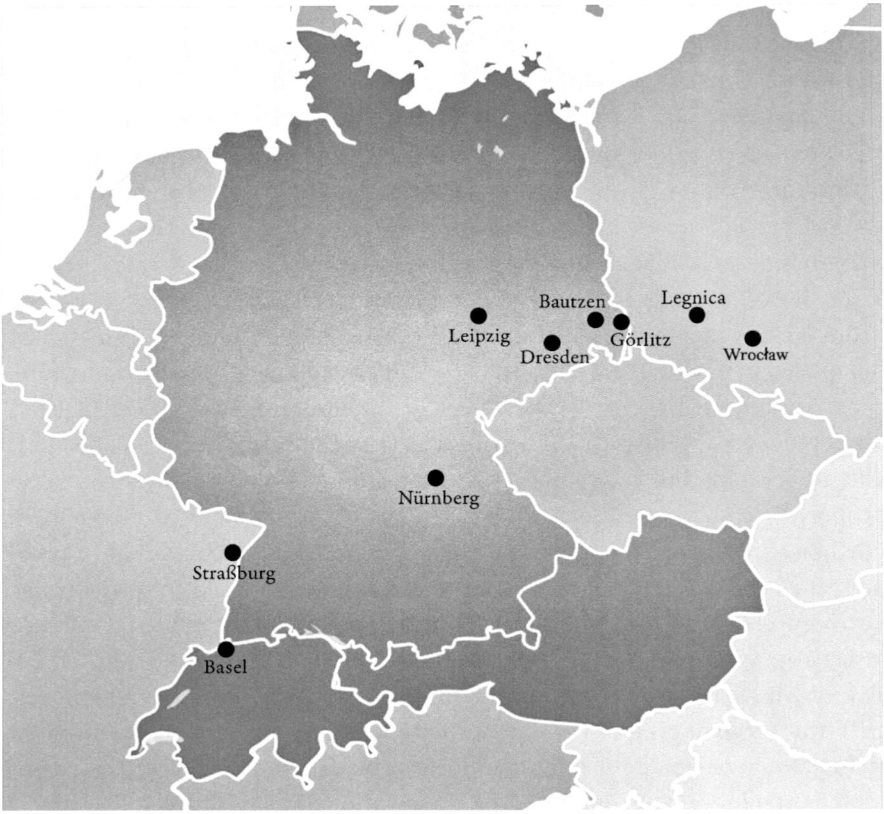

Figure 1.3. Map of Hans Bruckner's business destinations. Created by Johanna Eger based on https://commons.wikimedia.org/wiki/File:Europe_blank_laea_location_map.svg. Used with permission.

(for the locations of the aforementioned places, see fig. 1.3).[41] It is evident that Hans Bruckner made significant purchases at major trade fairs.[42] He can therefore be regarded as an intermediary between the large trade fairs and the smaller local markets. The merchant's book indicates that transactions of goods were not always settled in a direct manner, but rather through the use of instalment payments. It is also noteworthy that goods purchased in other cities and at major regional trade fairs were not paid for on the spot, but by instalments. Subsequently, the aforementioned payments were made at the next meetings. The merchants were confident that they would receive their remuneration.

41 Schulze, "Ein Krämerbuch aus dem Ende des 15. Jahrhunderts," 198–99.

42 Bruckner, *Krämerbuch*, fols. 41v–45r, 46v–49r, 52v–59r, 62r–63r, 64r–68r.

Upon his arrival in Görlitz, he initially leased a vault from his future brother-in-law, Michel Schmidt, for the sum of three Hungarian guilders per annum, thus enabling him to pursue his commercial activities.[43] In 1479, he at last purchased a permanent store.[44] It can be reasonably assumed that he had access to substantial financial resources to purchase this trading establishment, which was reserved exclusively for privileged Görlitz merchants. It seems probable that he was assisted by the inheritance paid to his wife by his brother-in-law between 1478 and 1480. The inheritance amounted to 185 mark groschen. In any case, Hans Bruckner was able to buy a shop between 1479 and 1483, paying a total of 140 mark groschen to the town.[45] There is considerable evidence suggesting that he operated this shop until 1496, at which point he either rented it out or ceased to run his business independently. Firstly, the merchant's book abruptly ceases, although there were still free pages available. Secondly, Hans Bruckner's general shop is no longer recorded as a merchant (Krämer) in the Görlitz land register, as was previously the case.[46] Moreover, Hans Bruckner had purchased a residence with stained glass windows in 1495, which he had already repaid a year later and which had cost 415 mark groschen.[47] It can be posited that Hans Bruckner was a successful merchant who was able to retire in his old age.

It would appear that Hans Bruckner had not concentrated his efforts on any one product. The range of goods offered by Hans Bruckner is diverse. Furthermore, the range of goods included high-quality items. The list of goods includes oil, flour, *Schmeer* (high-quality animal fat), sugar, honey, rice, almonds, nuts, figs, peach pits, grapes (sultanas and currants), saffron, pepper, nutmeg, mace, cloves, cinnamon, ginger, laurel, myrrh, thyme, roses, calamus (root of the water lily), caraway, white lead, copper, alum, sulphur, tartar, gall apples, and verdigris. The following textiles were identified: pitch, frankincense, galangal, curcuma, hellebore, liquorice, gold, canvas, coloured linen fabrics, twill, coloured cloth, English robes, Ulm and Augsburg barchent, coloured harras (light woollen fabric), coloured taffeta, shiny canvas, and zindel (silk taffeta). The list of materials includes wool, cotton, coloured twine, Köln silk, sewing silk, woad thread, spun gold and silver, bordure silk, braid, shingle braid, and cord. Additionally, the list includes a variety of

---

43 Schulze, "Ein Krämerbuch aus dem Ende des 15. Jahrhunderts," 182.

44 Bruckner, *Krämerbuch*, fols. 60r–61r.

45 Schulze, "Ein Krämerbuch aus dem Ende des 15. Jahrhunderts," 182.

46 Schulze, "Ein Krämerbuch aus dem Ende des 15. Jahrhunderts," 183.

47 Schulze, "Ein Krämerbuch aus dem Ende des 15. Jahrhunderts," 184.

skins and furs, flax, soap, wax, iron, window glass, wire, rods, lights, candlesticks, weights, jugs, vessels, sacks, mirrors, bath basins, gloves, bags (also decorated and of high quality), berets, trousers, collars, clasps, knives, light scissors, mouse traps, mortars, bowls, swords, bolts, paper, travel cots; gold rings, belts, pearls; painted cloths, painted figures, painted letters, compasses, and books.[48] However, the income generated from this investment is currently unknown. Hans Bruckner did not specialize in a single type of commodity, thereby diversifying his risk exposure. Moreover, he did not confine his activities to the trading of luxury goods, which is indicative of a similar approach. Nevertheless, his range did include luxury goods, for which the profit margins were undoubtedly considerable. The trading business of Hans Bruckner was not on the scale of that of long-distance merchants,[49] but it was undoubtedly a lucrative business for a wealthy merchant. In addition, he made an investment in mining concessions (Kuxe) in Bohemia, the purchase of which is recorded in the merchant's book with the stipulation of an instalment payment.[50]

The meticulous documentation of credit relationships not only serves to emphasize a heightened sense of obligation but also serves as a tangible manifestation of social and economic ties. Bruckner's merchant's book provides a detailed account of the intricate web of his trading network, emphasizing the enduring relationships that transcend mere financial transactions. This enduring record not only facilitated future dealings but also served as a testament to the enduring nature of commerce in his era. It not only sheds light on his extensive trading networks but also underscores the operational intricacies of his enterprise. His diverse range of goods and participation in regional trade fairs position him as a significant figure bridging local and broader markets. To manage his extensive (debt) transactions, Bruckner required a portable merchant's book, which he was able to keep. It is unclear whether he acquired these accounting practices through formal education or through experience.[51]

---

48 Compilation of the goods at Schulze, "Ein Krämerbuch aus dem Ende des 15. Jahrhunderts," 188–95.

49 See the introduction to this volume.

50 Bruckner, *Krämerbuch*, fols. 79r, 80r.

51 The research on the education of merchants is mostly based on accounting and merchants' books as well as merchants' letters, see Hammel-Kiesow, "Schriftlichkeit und Handelsgesellschaften niederdeutsch-hansischer und oberdeutscher Kaufleute," 213–41; Tophinke, *Handelstexte*, 90–112.

Bruckner's Merchant's Book: A Typical One?

Portability and Usability of Merchants' Books

It is now necessary to integrate this case study into a larger framework to draw conclusions about structural similarities from the individual case and thus answer the question about the convention of written accounting. The common research opinion is that the absence of a general standardized training programme or template for the collection of commercial information in manuscripts has resulted in a considerable degree of variation in the format of these merchants' books.[52] For example, Denzel describes these books as "documenting the occurrence of commercial transactions."[53] They are typically analyzed in research under various source terms, including account books, memorials, and diaries.[54]

One challenge in studying merchants' books is that they often contain more than just formalized content. Over time, writing concepts have evolved, and this type of bookkeeping in the fifteenth century led to books of mixed content. Hans Bruckner includes important commercial knowledge for his business in the form of documents and letters. This part plays a very subordinate role. The mixture of different forms of knowledge does not make them appear solely as account books or debt books. It is important to note that the type of merchants' books to which Bruckner's book belongs are characterized by their heterogeneity. Its function as a memory aid becomes clear when income, expenditure and debt relationships are written down,

52 This was met with the emergence of an increasing number of arithmetic schools as well as of arithmetical and merchant's manuals, which quickly went into print and contributed to the emergence of a standardization trend (Witthöft, "Handelspraktiken und Kaufmannschaft in Mittelalter und Neuzeit," 201–5). For an attempt to categorize merchants' account books from the fourteenth and fifteenth century as a separate text type, see fundamentally Tophinke, *Handelstexte*.

53 Denzel, "Handelspraktiken als wirtschaftshistorische Quellengattung," 11; Arlinghaus notes that in northern Europe, account books retained their notebook-like character well into the fifteenth century (Arlinghaus, *Zwischen Notiz und Bilanz*, 354).

54 The account book of Hinrik Dunkelgud, which spans the years 1479 to 1517, has been classified by archivists and researchers in disparate ways. In her recent study of the document, Sabrina Stockhusen refers to it as an account book. However, it has also been designated as a memorial book, a secret book, and a diary; Stockhusen, *Hinrik Dunkelgud und sein Rechnungsbuch*, 30; for further insight, see her comments on the issue of terminology and the references to further research provided therein (Stockhusen, *Hinrik Dunkelgud und sein Rechnungsbuch*, 30–31).

as well as any other useful information for the merchant.[55] The books facilitated the organization of long-term business relationships and even the establishment of trading companies. Furthermore, they could be employed in the context of legal disputes, which is evidenced by the recording of copies of deeds, wills, or house purchases.[56]

Although these books—which are known in Italian as *Ricordanze*—contain some family information, they are always related or mixed up with commercial and business information.[57] They should not directly be interpreted in the context of house and family books as occasionally suggested in research.[58] However, the two categories—merchants' books and family books—are united by the time and place of their creation. Furthermore, both types must be seen in the context of the spread of writing and the tendency to collect and record family and economic information, but the function of these two kinds of books is not the same. But both types of sources demonstrate that the domains of family and business were not yet distinct. Stockhusen elucidates the distinction between the two categories of text, which can be partially attributed to social categorization. The urban elite was able to maintain both house and family registers, as well as account books. In contrast, wealthy merchants who did not belong to the exclusive group of urban leaders did not maintain house and family registers but did keep account books in which family matters could be recorded. In contrast to the house and family registers of the elite, these family matters did not necessarily concern the significant stages of family life, such as births, marriages, and deaths. Instead, they pertained to matters that were closely linked to business matters, such as house purchases and wills.

From the aforementioned explanations, it is evident that the boundaries between merchants' books and family and house books are not fixed. This prompts the question of what constitutes sufficient family information for a

55 The function as a memory aid is also emphasized by Arlingshaus (Arlinghaus, *Zwischen Notiz und Bilanz*, 340–41) and the merchants were well aware of this. See the note in Ott Ruland's merchant's book: *Ich hab des namens vergessen*, Holbach, "Item das ich Ott Ruland ain kauf hab getroffen," 86.

56 Stockhusen, *Hinrik Dunkelgud und sein Rechnungsbuch*, 131–32; Additionally, Arlinghaus posits the potential legal function of account books (Arlinghaus, *Zwischen Notiz und Bilanz*, 342–48); and Mickwitz points out that the chances of the sources surviving are increased if they are used within a legal framework (Mickwitz, *Aus Revaler Handelsbüchern*, 10).

57 See Paul Schweitzer-Martin's chapter in this volume.

58 See Stockhusen, *Hinrik Dunkelgud und sein Rechnungsbuch*, 40–43.

book to be designated as a family book. This question also arises in a completely different area, where the transitions to urban chronicles and family books are also fluid.[59] It is evident that personal and family information was considered of such importance that it was inscribed in texts of—from a modern view—a completely different type. In this manner, personal and family information is connected to the town or business and inscribed in the memory of business transactions and social networks, as well as in urban histories. A more precise definition of the source genre merchant's book is necessary in order to differentiate it from other sources and to define the characteristics of the genre more precisely. Perhaps we can get a clearer picture if we include the materiality of the books in our considerations.

Bruckner's merchant's book is characterized by the changing layout, the non-linear bookkeeping system in place and the structurally unsystematic arrangement. This unambiguously defines the book as a sustained pragmatic text, distinct from a straightforward fair copy. In addition to these features, it is essential to consider its small size and weight, both of which are advantageous for transport. Furthermore, the limp binding makes it sturdy to close and protects it from moisture and mechanical damage; these are also characteristics that make the book resilient to the influences it was exposed to while travelling. Furthermore, the leather cover can be secured by means of an overlapping back cover.

Such bindings are described in (modern) library and archive catalogues as flexible leather or parchment bindings (in Latin: *liber sine asseribus*; in English: limp bindings).[60] These are bindings in which the book block is stitched directly into a flexible cover. The binding cords are readily discernible from the exterior, and the spine may be reinforced with materials such as wood, horn, or leather. In the case of Bruckner, the attached leather straps serve to reinforce and secure the binding. Furthermore, the front or back cover of numerous such bindings has been extended to form a flap. The term *Koperte* has become established in the German-speaking world as a designation for this type of binding.

The advantages of a limp binding in comparison to wooden and leather covers are readily apparent. Limp bindings are lightweight and flexible, yet offer protection, especially for the fore-edge. This protects the book

---

59 Bruch, "Die Darstellung genealogischen Wissens," 61–86.

60 See Ottermann, "Wege zu Koperten," 348, 355. The term was first introduced by Wieland Schmidt, who undertook research into this specific type of binding across a range of disciplines. This is a source term from the fourteenth century (*coopertorium*). (Schmidt, "In einem Kopert gebunden," 63–65).

all round and makes it easy to put in a bag or similar. Furthermore, these books are characterized by increased portability.[61] "The limp binding (*Koperte*) is suitable for all situations of travelling or permanent or temporary mobility, as it saves weight and provides complete book block protection."[62] It is conceivable that this type of binding was less expensive to manufacture and could be more readily constructed by individuals without specialized training and binding tools.[63] It seems unlikely that this factor played any role in the Bruckner book, which was lavishly and meticulously decorated.

The surviving copies from the early and high Middle Ages indicate a favoured use for the pastoral care of congregations (exegetical and catechetical texts and collections of sermons). This type of binding was also used for books of private piety (Psalters, prayer books) and for books for teaching (grammar, rhetoric, vocabulary).[64] So far, it is mainly books from libraries and from the early and high Middle Ages that have been analyzed. It is important to note that limp bindings were more susceptible to deterioration than wooden and leather bindings,[65] yet a review of the archives, which also contain books in limp bindings, provides a more comprehensive understanding. In addition to the books from the fields of pastoral care, teaching, and private piety, there is also the everyday, pragmatic writing such as merchants' books, notebooks, and manuals.[66] The binding, the size, and the open layout of Bruckner's book make it a portable book. As an artifact, the book already defines the function for contemporaries and, in the present day, provides us with clues about its use. This is evidenced

---

61 Scholla, "Libri sine asseribus," 276–77; Ottermann, "Wege zu Koperten," 355.

62 Scholla, "Libri sine asseribus," 277. The existence of portable books with wooden covers in a small format (e.g., *Perlbibeln*) does not detract from this characteristic; on the contrary, the copies were not crafted for a representative purpose.

63 Scholla, "Libri sine asseribus," 276–77. One example is the sixteenth-century copert binding in quarto format, which cost three batzen. A leather-covered wooden cover cost between seven and nine batzen; Brinkhus, "Koperte, die Vielfalt des Unscheinbaren," 76; Knaus, "Hochmittelalterliche Koperteinbände," 335.

64 Scholla, "Libri sine asseribus," 277.

65 Ottermann, "Wege zu Koperten," 355–57.

66 My own research has enabled me to add to the list of portable books that were bound as copies an account book from the thirteenth and fourteenth centuries from the Cistercian visitation context (Bruch, *Die Zisterze Kaisheim*), as well as a book with craft knowledge on bell, well, and gun casting, and on fireworks and war and craft machines from 1524. Both were carried around, albeit for different reasons (Bruch, "Transmission," 35–58).

by the examination of the material properties. It is now time to place other books by merchants from the late Middle Ages alongside the case study as a comparative foil.

A Typology of Merchants' Books in Late Medieval German-Speaking Lands

A comprehensive comparative analysis of merchants' books from the fourteenth to sixteenth century has yet to be conducted. Nevertheless, it is essential to ascertain which books were portable and which were not, thereby establishing a systematic approach. It is evident that this cannot be achieved in a single chapter; however, the objective is to illustrate the initial approaches that differentiate merchants' books and to demonstrate that there was a subcategory of transportable merchants' books whose functions extended beyond those of immobile books. In the following analysis, I have used the merchants' books that have been studied and mostly edited by other scholars as a basis for comparison.[67] I am conscious of the fact that a significant body of source material from German-speaking countries has yet to be discovered or subjected to exhaustive analysis and that it currently resides in archives awaiting examination. This study represents the inaugural attempt to examine this genre of sources in depth.

The methodology employed in this study combines critical content analysis and codicological analysis, viewing the manuscripts as expressions of a specific written culture within which merchants operated. By examining the content and materiality of these manuscripts, insights into the functionality and significance of portable books in economic and social networks are gained. Two aspects that interact with each other are of particular significance in this context: firstly, the function of the surviving books for the writing merchants must be explored. Secondly, the materiality of the books must be considered, as this can provide insights into how they were used and functioned in the past. This is because the writing merchants employed a variety of book formats and designs with the intention of ensuring optimal functionality.

---

67 A number of research overviews have been produced which bring together the surviving sources and categorize the associated research. With regard to German merchant books, see Steinbrink, *Ulrich Meltinger*, 18–20, while for Italian merchant books, see Lang, *Wirtschaften*, 76–90. Lang also brings together the Italian and German research traditions.

Table 1.1. Fifteenth-century merchants' books.

Format	Dimensions (mm)	Fols.	Binding	Index	Main Function
HANS BRUCKNER (Görlitz 1476–1496)					
4°	165 × 225 × 25	92	limp	yes	debt register
ULRICH MELTINGER[68] (Basel 1466–1494)					
2°	—[69]	376	limp	yes	main book
JOHAN PYRE[70] (Gdansk 1421–1454)					
Schmal-folio	150 × 420 × 65	113	limp[71]	no	main book
HINRIK DUNKELGUD[72] (Lübeck 1479–1517)					
2°	230 × 293	234	limp	no	debts, goods
STEFFAN MAIGNOW[73] (Konstanz 1477–1501)					
2°	210 × 295	167	limp	yes	family, business
LUDWIG KILCHMANN[74] (Basel 1484–1518)					
kl. 2°	—	350	hard	yes	debts, family, chronicle
JOHANN SLOESGIN[75] (Köln 1422–1468)					
2°	—	96	hard	no	debts, family, business
HERMANN WARENDORP and **JOHANN CLINGENBERG**[76] (Lübeck 1330–1336)					
4°	155 × 230	24	limp	no	justification of substitute business

68 Steinbrink, *Ulrich Meltinger*, 51–55; also 211–530.

69 Em dashes denote where information is missing in the catalogue.

70 Orłowska, *Johan Pyre*, 24, 34–42; text edited in Orłowska.

71 It can be reasonably assumed that the book was not initially bound in its present form; rather, it is likely that it was expanded and subsequently bound during its period of use (Orłowska, *Johan Pyre*, 25).

72 Stockhusen, *Hinrik Dunkelgud und sein Rechnungsbuch*, 133–40; Roover, "The Development of Accounting," 174; edition: Stockhusen, *Hinrik Dunkelgud und sein Rechnungsbuch*, 241–350.

73 Signori and Müntz, *Das Geschäftsbuch des Konstanzer Goldschmiedes Steffan Maignow*, xi, xv–xvii, xxvii; text edited in Signori and Müntz, *Das Geschäftsbuch des Konstanzer Goldschmiedes Steffan Maignow*, 3–111.

74 Signori, *Das Schuldbuch des Basler Kaufmanns Ludwig Kilchmann*, 29–30; text edited in Signori, *Das Schuldbuch des Basler Kaufmanns Ludwig Kilchmann*, 37–116.

75 Seidel, *Freunde und Verwandte*; Herborn, "Bürgerliches Selbstverständnis im spätmittelalterlichen Köln," 490–520.

76 Tophinke, *Handelstexte*, 126–33; Rörig, "Das älteste erhaltene deutsche Kaufmannsbüchlein," 167–215.

Format	Dimensions (mm)	Fols.	Binding	Index	Main Function
JOHANN TÖLNER the Younger[77] (Rostock 1345–1350)					
2°	210 × 295	29	rebound	no	company business, business
HERMANN and **JOHANN WITTENBORG**[78] (Lübeck 1329–1360)					
2°	215–30 × 290–310	40	limp	no	debts, goods
FREDERICUS (Vicko) VON GELDERN[79] (Hamburg 1367–1392)					
2°	220 × 300	84	limp	no	accounts, pensions, debts
JOHANN VAN NUYSS and DIETMAR BUNGERT (Köln 1427–1434)					
Doppel-folio	—	28	unbound	no	monitoring the joint commercial transactions
PAUL MULICH[80] (Nürnberg 1495)					
Schmal-folio	105 mm × 325 mm	120	limp	no	goods available in Lübeck and the goods he purchased at the Fastenmesse in Frankfurt am Main and sent to Lübeck
MARKUS and HANS POPPLAU[81] (Wrocław 1502–1516)					
2[82]	230 × 330 × 50	150	rebound	?	company, debts, cash sales
WILHELM and MATTHÄUS RUTINGER[83] (Regensburg 1383–1407)					
2°	225 × 295	520	limp	no	main book
OTT RULAND[84] (Ulm 1444–1458)					
4°	145 × 212	96	rebound	no	company, debts, accounts

77 Tophinke, *Handelstexte*, 133–36; Koppmann, *Johan Tölners Handlungsbuch von 1345–1350.*

78 Tophinke, *Handelstexte*, 139–47, Mollwo, *Das Handlungsbuch von Hermann und Johann Wittenborg.*

79 Tophinke, *Handelstexte*, 147–61; Nirrnheim, *Das Handlungsbuch Vickos von Geldersen.*

80 Tophinke, *Handelstexte*, 184–86; Rörig, "Das Einkaufsbüchlein der Nürnberg-Lübecker Mulichs," 288–350.

81 Petry, *Die Popplau*, 4–26.

82 Destroyed during the Second World War. I would like to thank Remigiusz Kazimierczak, Deputy Director of the State Archives in Wrocław, for the helpful information.

83 Bastian, *Das Runtingerbuch 1383–1407 und verwandtes Material*, vol. 1: *Darstellung*; Bastian, *Das Runtingerbuch 1383–1407 und verwandtes Material*, vol. 2: *Text des Runtingerbuches.*

84 Bastian, *Das Runtingerbuch 1383–1407 und verwandtes Material*, vol. 1: *Darstellung*, 238–46; 293–309; Holbach, "'Item das ich Ott Ruland ain kauf hab getroffen,'" 81–98; Konrad D., *Ott Rulands Handlungsbuch.*

Format	Dimensions (mm)	Fols.	Binding	Index	Main Function
HOLZSCHUHER[85] (Nürnberg 1304–1307)					
4°	170 × 235	51[86]	hard	no	debts
HANS and PETER LERER[87] (München 1440–1458)					
Schmal-folio	—	90	rebound	no	accounts from trade fairs, tax lists
PETER DRACH[88] (Speyer 1480–1503)					
2°	210 × 280	90	fragment	no	list of goods, accounts, debts, contracts

In the case study presented, it is evident that the contents are of interest to a travelling trader, who carries his entire debt network with him and can call it up at any time. The layout is designed for rapid reference, although the potential of this has not been fully exploited by the scribe. The entries serve as a memory aid and, at the same time, a visible manifestation of social and economic networks. It is possible that Hans Bruckner kept another, non-portable merchant's book, which remained in his shop in Görlitz. Bruckner was distinguished by his frequent travel and trade at fairs and in other cities. The addressee of the book, who in this case is identical to the scribe, also plays an essential role in the interpretation and typologization of the books. Despite the perceived disadvantages of portability, such as vulnerability to damage or loss, the advantages in terms of accessibility and utility outweighed these concerns.

In order to situate these results within the broader corpus of contemporary merchants' books and to provide an overview of the known and edited merchants' books, I have prepared a table (table 1.1) with the following information: the books, their scribes, their chronological location, and, finally, the material characteristics relevant to the investigation.[89] A comparative analy-

85 Chroust and Proesler, *Das Handlungsbuch der Holzschuher*, ix–xi; Chroust and Proesler, *Das Handlungsbuch der Holzschuher*, 1–120.

86 Parchment.

87 Schwab, *Das Münchner Lererbuch*, 333–40; Schwab, *Das Lererbuch*.

88 Mäkeler, *Das Rechnungsbuch des Speyerer Druckherrn Peter Drach d. M.*; Schweitzer-Martin, *Kooperation und Innovation im Speyerer Buchdruck*; text edited in Geldner, "Das Rechnungsbuch des Speyrer Druckherrn, Verlegers und Großbuchhändlers Peter Drach," 1–196; Wunderle, *Die mittelalterlichen Handschriften der Studienbibliothek Dillingen*, 417–20.

89 It should be noted that the list is not intended to be exhaustive. However, it does provide a comprehensive overview of the most frequently referenced books in academic research. Merchants' books that have survived only in fragments and

sis reveals that the majority of the analyzed merchants' books are bound in a relatively flimsy manner. This type of binding appears to be the conventional choice for pragmatic writing by merchants. Most of the books are in folio format, with Bruckner's book being particularly noteworthy for its use of the quarto format. Additionally, a small number of the books are in the narrow folio format. Both the books in quarto format (with limp binding) and the books in narrow folio format (with limp binding) are designed to be portable.[90] It is also necessary to consider the fact that books in hardcover (Sloesgin) and those with large numbers in folio format are not designed for transportation (Meltinger). The heterogeneity and hybridity of the books in question does not necessarily imply that they were also carried around. It is only through the examination of the material analysis that conclusions can be drawn regarding the portability of the books in question.

A comparison of the functions shows merchants' books can assume a multitude of roles. They function as account books, serving as statements of account for a trading company or a proxy. They serve as debt registers to maintain an overview of outstanding debts and obligations, to facilitate settlement and redemption, and to record, consolidate, and reactivate the debt network as a social network. In the event of a legal dispute, both types of merchants' books can serve as evidence. However, merchants' books can also be used to document the total volume of business, often in the form of so-called ledgers, which have been handed down in plain copy and are available for consultation. Furthermore, merchants' books may simultaneously serve all of the aforementioned functions and additionally function as memorials for family news, copies of documents, privileges, and so forth. It is, therefore, possible for a single volume to serve multiple functions, effectively acting as a comprehensive repository for a variety of purposes. The functional overlap of these books makes their interpretation and typology challenging. This is further complicated by the fact that, in the majority of cases, only a single book belonging to a given merchant has survived to the present day. Consequently, the available evidence is often limited to a small

---

without an assigned scribe, such as the thirteenth-century Kiel fragment edited by Korlén, were not included (Korlén, "Kieler Bruchstücke kaufmännischer Buchführung am Ende des 13. Jahrhunderts," 102–12; Brandt, "Ein Stück kaufmännischer Buchführung aus dem letzten Viertel des 13. Jahrhunderts," 308–35). It should be noted that female writers also contributed to the corpus of books for merchants; see Schmid, *Schreiben für Status*, 98–99.

90 Bischoff, *Paläographie*, 45; Bastian, *Das Runtingerbuch 1383–1407 und verwandtes Material*, vol. 1: *Darstellung*, 240.

section of the system of merchants' books. These types of books are to be understood as part of a much more complex accounting system, which usually comprised loose slips of paper and several books with different functions that were kept at the same time. Though, it is rare for more than one of these books to survive for a merchant in the fifteenth century in the region north of the Alps.[91] However, there are exceptions to this rule. The most prominent examples in the German-speaking world are the merchants' books of the Veckinchusen family from Lübeck[92] and the merchants' books from Tallin.[93]

The differentiation of the account books based on their material appearance for the Datini/di Berto trading company, as proposed by Franz Arlinghaus, can be corroborated here. The main account books are immobile, with a strong leather binding and a cover enclosing the front edge (measuring 300 mm × 410 mm). The smaller books (*Ricordanze*, memorials, income and expenditure books, etc.) measure 225 mm × 300 mm and are bound in parchment. Arlinghaus posits that the significance and longevity of the account books can be discerned from their material composition.[94] We can add to

---

91 Stockhusen, *Hinrik Dunkelgud und sein Rechnungsbuch*, 31–32. The examples of the Datini and Lang for the Salviati and Welser demonstrate the extensive nature of bookkeeping, particularly in Italy, and the types of books that constituted it (Lang, *Wirtschaften*; Arlinghaus, *Zwischen Notiz und Bilanz*).

92 Thirteen merchants' books kept by Hildebrand Veckchinhusen himself have survived (plus 580 other documents, mainly letters and these were sent to him by his brother Sivert in particular); Cordes, *Spätmittelalterlicher Gesellschaftshandel im Hanseraum*, 235–37; Lenz, "Äußere Beschreibung der Bücher," xli–xlv; editions: Lesnikov, Stark, and Cordes, *Die Handelsbücher des Hildebrand Veckinchusen*; Lesnikov, *Die Handelsbücher des hansischen Kaufmanns Veckinchusen*.

93 The merchants from Tallinn kept books as main books (*caput*), debt accounts, and farmers' books (*Bauernbücher*; containing lists of outstanding debts). These books have not been edited, but have been partially digitized and are certainly worthy of further analysis, especially as there is an account book in Tallinn that was printed several times and describes a specific accounting system (Mickwitz, *Aus Revaler Handelsbüchern*, 188–205). Merchants with several books include: Helmich Ficke (Tallinna Linnaarhiiv, TLA.230.1.Af17, 22, 25, 28, 32–35, 38), Jasper Kappenberg (Tallinna Linnaarhiiv, TLA.230.1.Af40, 41, 46/I, 46/II, 46/III, 46/IV, Bh21/1, 21/III,), Bernt Pal (Tallinna Linnaarhiiv, TLA.230.1.Af18) Steffen Pelser (Tallinna Linnaarhiiv, TLA.230.1.Af19, 20, Bh35/II, 35/III), Johann Selhorst (Tallinna Linnaarhiiv, TLA.230.1.Af21, 23, Bh5/1, 5/II), Tönnis Smith (Tallinna Linnaarhiiv, TLA.230.1.Af42–44), Matheus Spielmann (Tallinna Linnaarhiiv, TLA.230.1.Af47, 48), Gotke van Techten (Tallinna Linnaarhiiv, TLA.230.1.Af16), Lütke von Menden (Tallinna Linnaarhiiv, TLA.230.1.Af29, 30, 31).

94 Arlinghaus, *Zwischen Notiz und Bilanz*, 137–40.

this the further proposition that smaller, more ephemeral books offered the advantage of being portable.

Conclusion

In conclusion, the results of a single case study were used as a basis for typologizing a source category. It was demonstrated that the classification of the books is dependent on both content and materiality. It has been shown that merchants' books, which are portable, can contain social information and that this information is available to the merchant, who is often very mobile, from any location. It has been demonstrated that merchants' books provided a form of materialized social network accompanying their merchant owners. Furthermore, although the books were often handed down individually, they were, in fact, just part of a network involving other books and written records. This network of records and books had functions that could overlap and were interdependent. Consequently, small, ephemeral books that could be carried around were capable of carrying information that could then be transferred to stationary books. The research field of merchants' books remains incomplete. A more extensive comparative study is required to expand upon the results presented here. However, Bruckner's book has demonstrated the wealth of information that contemporary research, which integrates economic and social-historical inquiries with cultural-historical methodologies, can yield.

Bibliography

Manuscript and Archival Sources

Görlitz, Ratsarchiv/Stadtarchiv, *Varia 70.*

Görlitz, Stadtarchiv, *Liber actorum 1478–1483*, fol. 19v.

Tallinna Linnaarhiiv, TLA.230.1.Af16–23, 25, 28–35, 38, 40–44, 46–48, Bh5/1, 5/II, 21/1, 21/III, 35/II, 35/III.

Printed Primary Sources

Bastian, Franz. *Das Runtingerbuch 1383–1407 und verwandtes Material zum Regensburger-südostdeutschen Handel und Münzwesen*. vol. 2: *Text des Runtingerbuches*. Deutsche Handelsakten des Mittelalters und der Neuzeit 7. Regensburg: Bosse, 1935.

Chroust, Anton and Hans Proesler, eds. *Das Handlungsbuch der Holzschuher in Nürnberg von 1304–1307*. Veröffentlichungen der Gesellschaft für Fränkische Geschichte 10. Erlangen: Palm & Enke, 1934.

Geldner, Ferdinand. "Das Rechnungsbuch des Speyrer Druckherrn, Verlegers und Großbuchhändlers Peter Drach." *Archiv für Geschichte des Buchwesens* 5 (1964): 1–196.

Haßler, Konrad D. *Ott Rulands Handlungsbuch*. Stuttgart: Literarischer Verein, 1843.

Koppmann, Karl. *Johan Tölners Handlungsbuch von 1345–1350*. Geschichtsquellen der Stadt Rostock 1. Rostock: Werthers, 1885.

Kuske, Bruno. *Quellen zur Geschichte des Kölner Handels und Verkehrs im Mittelalter*. vol. 4: *Besondere Quellengruppen des späteren Mittelalters: Register*. Publikationen der Gesellschaft für Rheinische Geschichtskunde 33. Bonn: Hanstein, 1934.

Lesnikov, Michail P., ed. *Die Handelsbücher des hansischen Kaufmanns Veckinchusen*. Forschungen zur mittelalterlichen Geschichte 19. Berlin: Akademie, 1973.

Lesnikov, Michail P., Walter Stark, and Albrecht Cordes, eds. *Die Handelsbücher des Hildebrand Veckinchusen: Kontobücher und übrige Manuale*. Quellen und Darstellungen zur hansischen Geschichte 67. Köln: Böhlau, 2013.

Mollwo, Karl. *Das Handlungsbuch von Hermann und Johann Wittenborg*. Leipzig: Dyksche,1901.

Nirrnheim, Hans. *Das Handlungsbuch Vickos von Geldersen*. Hamburg: Voss, 1895.

Orłowska, Anna Paulina. *Johan Pyre: Ein Kaufmann und sein Handelsbuch im spätmittelalterlichen Danzig: Darstellung und Edition*. Quellen und Darstellungen zur Hansischen Geschichte 77. Köln: Böhlau, 2022.

Schwab, Ingo. *Das Lererbuch: Ein Münchner Kaufmannsbuch des 15. Jahrhunderts*. Materialien zur bayerischen Landesgeschichte 18. München: Bayerische Akademie der Wissenschaften, 2005.

Signori, Gabriela. *Das Schuldbuch des Basler Kaufmanns Ludwig Kilchmann (gest. 1518)*. Vierteljahrschrift für Sozial- und Wirtschaftsgeschichte: Beihefte 231. Stuttgart: Steiner, 2014.

Signori, Gabriela, and Marc Müntz, eds. *Das Geschäftsbuch des Konstanzer Goldschmiedes Steffan Maignow*. Konstanzer Geschichts- und Rechtsquellen 42. Ostfildern: Thorbecke, 2012.

Steinbrink, Matthias. *Ulrich Meltinger: Ein Basler Kaufmann am Ende des 15. Jahrhunderts*. Vierteljahrschrift für Sozial- und Wirtschaftsgeschichte 197. Stuttgart: Steiner, 2007.

Stockhusen, Sabrina. *Hinrik Dunkelgud und sein Rechnungsbuch (1479 bis 1517): Lebensformen eines Lübecker Krämers an der Wende vom 15. zum 16. Jahrhundert.* Vierteljahrschrift für Sozial- und Wirtschaftsgeschichte 245. Stuttgart: Steiner, 2019.

Secondary Works

Arlinghaus, Franz-Josef. *Zwischen Notiz und Bilanz: Zur Eigendynamik des Schriftgebrauchs in der kaufmännischen Buchführung am Beispiel der Datini/ di Berto-Handelsgesellschaft in Avignon (1367–1373)*. Gesellschaft, Kultur und Schrift. Mediävistische Beiträge 8. Frankfurt am Main: Lang, 2000.

Bastian, Franz. *Das Runtingerbuch 1383–1407 und verwandtes Material zum Regensburger-südostdeutschen Handel und Münzwesen*. vol. 1: *Darstellung*. Deutsche Handelsakten des Mittelalters und der Neuzeit 6. Regensburg: Bosse, 1944.

Bischoff, Bernhard. *Paläographie des römischen Altertums und des abendländischen Mittelalters*. 4th ed. Grundlagen der Germanistik 24. Berlin: Schmidt, 2009.

Brandt, Ahasver von. "Ein Stück kaufmännischer Buchführung aus dem letzten Viertel des 13. Jahrhunderts. Aufzeichnungen aus dem Detailgeschäft eines Lübecker Gewandschneiders." In *Lübeck, Hanse, Nordeuropa. Gedächtnisschrift für Ahasver von Brandt*. Edited by Klaus Friedland and Rolf Sprandel, 308–35. Köln: Böhlau, 1979.

Brinkhus, Gerd. "Koperte, die Vielfalt des Unscheinbaren: Die flexiblen Bucheinbände der Bibliotheca Amploniana." In *Der Schatz des Amplonius: Die große Bibliothek des Mittelalters in Erfurt*. Edited by Kathrin Paasch and Döbler Eckehart, 76–83. Erfurt: Stadt- und Regionalbibliothek, 2001.

Bruch, Julia. "Die Darstellung genealogischen Wissens in von Handwerker:innen geschriebenen Chroniken des 16. und 17. Jahrhunderts." In *Genealogisches Wissen in Mittelalter und Früher Neuzeit: Konstruktion—Darstellung—Rezeption*. Edited by Giuseppe Cusa and Thomas Dorfner, 61–86. Cultures and Practices of Knowledge in History 16. Berlin: De Gruyter, 2023.

——. "Transmission of Useful Knowledge in Texts Written by Craftsmen: Two Case Studies from the Holy Roman Empire." In *L'economia della conoscenza: Innovazione, produttività e crescita economica, secc. XIII–XVIII / The Knowledge Economy: Innovation, Productivity and Economic Growth, 13th to 18th Century*. Edited by Giampiero Nigro, 35–58. Datini Studies in Economic History 3. Firenze: Firenze University Press, 2023.

——. *Die Zisterze Kaisheim und ihre Tochterklöster: Studien zur Organisation und zum Wirtschaften spätmittelalterlicher Frauenklöster mit einer Edition des "Kaisheimer Rechnungsbuches."* Vita regularis. Editionen 5. Berlin: LIT, 2013.

Cordes, Albrecht. *Spätmittelalterlicher Gesellschaftshandel im Hanseraum*. Quellen und Darstellungen zur Hansischen Geschichte 45. Köln: Böhlau, 1998.

Denzel, Markus A. "Handelspraktiken als wirtschaftshistorische Quellengattung vom Mittelalter bis in das frühe 20. Jahrhundert: Eine Einführung." In *Kaufmannsbücher und Handelspraktiken vom Spätmittelalter bis zum beginnenden 20. Jahrhundert = Merchant's Books and Mercantile "Pratiche" from the Late Middle Ages to the Beginning of the 20th Century*. Edited by Markus A. Denzel, Jean Claude Hocquet, and Harald Witthöft, 11–45. Vierteljahrschrift für Sozial- und Wirtschaftsgeschichte 163. Stuttgart: Steiner, 2002.

Grimm, Heinrich. "Die Buchführer des deutschen Kulturbereichs und ihre Niederlassungsorte in der Zeitspanne 1490 bis um 1550." *Archiv für die Geschichte des Buchwesens* 7 (1965): 1154–1771.

Hammel-Kiesow, Rolf. "Schriftlichkeit und Handelsgesellschaften niederdeutsch-hansischer und oberdeutscher Kaufleute im späten 13. und im 14. Jahrhundert." In *Von Nowgorod bis London: Studien zu Handel, Wirtschaft und Gesellschaft im mittelalterlichen Europa: Festschrift für Stuart Jenks zum 60. Geburtstag*. Edited by Marie-Luise Heckmann and Jens Röhrkasten, 213–41. Göttingen: Vandenhoeck & Ruprecht, 2008.

Herborn, Wolfgang. "Bürgerliches Selbstverständnis im spätmittelalterlichen Köln: Bemerkungen zu zwei Hausbüchern aus der ersten Hälfte des 15. Jahrhunderts." In *Die Stadt in der europäischen Geschichte. Festschrift Edith Ennen*. Edited by Werner Besch et al., 490–520. Bonn: Röhrscheid, 1972.

Hirschbiegel, Jan, Stefanie von Welser, and Angelika Westermann, eds. *Ökonomisch bestimmtes Handeln in der Vormoderne: Eine Frage des Vertrauens?* Neunhofer Dialog 4. Husum: Matthiesen, 2021.

Holbach, Rudolf. "'Item das ich Ott Ruland ain kauf hab getroffene": Zu den Handelsgeschäften des Ulmer Kaufmanns im 15. Jahrhundert." In *"Kopet uns werk by tyden": Beiträge zur hansischen und preußischen Geschichte: Walter Stark zum 75. Geburtstag*. Edited by Nils Jörn, Detlef Kattinger, and Horst Wernicke, 81–98. Schwerin: Helms, 1999.

Irsigler, Franz. "Leben und Werk eines spätmittelalterlichen Kaufmanns am Beispiel von Johann van Nuyss aus Köln." *Jahrbuch des Kölnischen Geschichtsvereins* 42 (1968): 103–36.

Jahnke, Carsten. "Bernd Pal, ein Kaufmann des 15. Jahrhunderts: Eine biographische Skizze." *Vana Tallinn* 15 (2004): 158–76.

Jecht, Richard. *Quellen zur Geschichte der Stadt Görlitz bis 1600*. Görlitz: Magistrat, 1909.

Knaus, Hermann. "Hochmittelalterliche Koperteinbände." *Zeitschrift für Bibliothekswesen und Bibliographie* 8 (1961): 326–36.

Korlén, Gustav. "Kieler Bruchstücke kaufmännischer Buchführung am Ende des 13. Jahrhunderts." *Niederdeutsche Mitteilungen* 5 (1949): 102–12.

Kypta, Ulla. "Classification/Types." In *Methods in Premodern Economic History: Case Studies from the Holy Roman Empire, c. 1300–c. 1600*. Edited by Ulla Kypta, Julia Bruch, and Tanja Skambraks, 401–3. Basingstoke: Palgrave Macmillan, 2019.

Lang, Heinrich. *Wirtschaften als kulturelle Praxis: Die Florentiner Salviati und die Augsburger Welser auf den Märkten in Lyon (1507–1559)*. Vierteljahrschrift für Sozial- und Wirtschaftsgeschichte 248. Stuttgart: Steiner, 2020.

Lenz, Wilhelm. "Äußere Beschreibung der Bücher." In *Die Handelsbücher des Hildebrand Veckinchusen: Kontobücher und übrige Manuale*. Edited by Michail P. Lesnikov, Walter Stark, and Albrecht Cordes, xli–xlv. Quellen und Darstellungen zur hansischen Geschichte 67. Köln: Böhlau, 2013.

Mähnert, Joachim and Stephan Selzer, eds. *Vertraute Ferne: Kommunikation und Mobilität im Hanseraum*. Husum: Husum, 2012.

Mäkeler, Hendrik. *Das Rechnungsbuch des Speyerer Druckherrn Peter Drach d. M. (um 1450–1504)*. Sachüberlieferung und Geschichte 38. St. Katharinen: Scripta Mercaturae, 2005.

Mickwitz, Gunnar. *Aus Revaler Handelsbüchern: Zur Technik des Ostseehandels in der ersten Hälfte des 16. Jahrhunderts*. Commentationes humanarum litterarum 9. Helsingfors: Akademische Buchhandlung, 1938.

Ottermann, Annelen. "Wege zu Koperten: Eine Orientierung am Beispiel der Stadtbibliothek Mainz." *Gutenberg-Jahrbuch* 76 (2001): 348–64.

Petry, Ludwig. *Die Popplau: Eine schlesische Kaufmannsfamilie des 15. und 16. Jahrhunderts*. Wrocław: Marcus, 1935.

Roover, Raymond de. "The Development of Accounting Prior to Luca Pacioli According to the Account Books of Medieval Merchants." In *Business, Banking, and Economic Thought in Late Medieval and Early Modern Europe: Selected Studies*. Edited by Julius Kirshner, 119–80. Chicago: University of Chicago Press, 1974.

Rörig, Fritz. "Das älteste erhaltene deutsche Kaufmannsbüchlein." In *Die Wirtschaftskräfte im Mittelalter: Abhandlungen zur Stadt- und Hansegeschichte*. Edited by Paul Kaegbein, 167–215. Wien: Böhlau, 1971.

——. "Das Einkaufsbüchlein der Nürnberg-Lübecker Mulichs auf der Frankfurter Fastenmesse des Jahres 1495." In *Die Wirtschaftskräfte im Mittelalter: Abhandlungen zur Stadt- und Hansegeschichte*. Edited by Paul Kaegbein, 288–350. Wien: Böhlau, 1971.

Schmid, Barbara. *Schreiben für Status und Herrschaft: Deutsche Autobiographik in Spätmittelalter und früher Neuzeit*. Zürich: Chronos, 2006.

Schmidt, Wieland. "In einem Kopert gebunden." In *Aus der Arbeit des Bibliothekars: Aufsätze und Abhandlungen: Fritz Redenbacher zum 60. Geburtstag dargebracht*. Edited by Bernhard Sinogowitz, 59–82. Schriften der Universitätsbibliothek Erlangen 4. Erlangen: Universitäts-Bibliothek, 1960.

Scholla, Agnes Bettina Hokyong. "Libri sine asseribus: Zur Einbandtechnik, Form und Inhalt mitteleuropäischer Koperte des 8. bis 14. Jahrhunderts." PhD diss., Universiteit Leiden, 2002.

Schulze, E. "Ein Krämerbuch aus dem Ende des 15. Jahrhunderts." *Neues Lausitzisches Magazin* 73 (1897): 181–201.

Schwab, Ingo. "Das Münchner Lererbuch." In *Netzwerke im europäischen Handel des Mittelalters*. Edited by Gerhard Fouquet and Hans-Jörg Gilomen, 333–40. Ostfildern: Thorbecke, 2010.

Schweitzer-Martin, Paul. *Kooperation und Innovation im Speyerer Buchdruck des ausgehenden Mittelalters*. Materiale Textkulturen 37. Berlin: De Gruyter, 2022.

Schweitzer-Martin, Paul. "Material und Format liturgischer Inkunabeldrucke: Eine Fallstudie zur Offizin Johannes Sensenschmidt." In *Wissen und Buchgestalt*. Edited by Philipp Hegel and Michael Krewet, 301–22. Episteme in Bewegung: Beiträge zu einer transdisziplinären Wissensgeschichte 26. Wiesbaden: Harrassowitz, 2022.

Seidel, Kerstin. *Freunde und Verwandte: Soziale Beziehungen in einer spätmittelalterlichen Stadt*. Campus historische Studien 49. Frankfurt am Main: Campus, 2009.

Skambraks, Tanja. "Die moralische Ökonomie des steirischen Kaufmanns Clemens Körbler (1500–1566/67)." In *Von unbequemen Dominikanern, organisierten Handwerkern und gefertigten Dingen: Festschrift für Sabine von Heusinger zum 60. Geburtstag*. Edited by Julia Bruch, Eva-Maria Cersovsky, and Andreas Lehnertz. Mittelalter. Interdisziplinäre Forschung und Rezeptionsgeschichte: Beihefte 5. https://mittelalter.hypotheses.org/34601.

——. "Tally Sticks as Media of Knowledge in the Contexts of Medieval Economic and Administrative History." In *L'economia della conoscenza: Innovazione, produttività e crescita economica, secc. XIII–XVIII / The Knowledge Economy: Innovation, Productivity and Economic Growth, 13th to 18th Century*. Edited by Giampiero Nigro, 137–58. Firenze: Firenze University Press, 2023.

Tophinke, Doris. *Handelstexte: Zu Textualität und Typik kaufmännischer Rechnungsbücher im Hanseraum des 14. und 15. Jahrhunderts*. ScriptOralia 114. Tübingen: Narr, 1999.

Witthöft, Harald. "Handelspraktiken und Kaufmannschaft in Mittelalter und Neuzeit: Rechnen und Schreiben mit Zahlen; Resümee und Perspektiven." In *Kaufmannsbücher und Handelspraktiken vom Spätmittelalter bis zum beginnenden 20. Jahrhundert = Merchant's Books and Mercantile "Pratiche" from the Late Middle Ages to the Beginning of the 20th Century*. Edited by Markus A. Denzel, Jean Claude Hocquet, and Harald Witthöft, 197–217. Vierteljahrschrift für Sozial- und Wirtschaftsgeschichte 163. Stuttgart: Steiner, 2002.

Wunderle, Elisabeth. *Die mittelalterlichen Handschriften der Studienbibliothek Dillingen*. Wiesbaden: Harrassowitz, 2006.

Chapter 2

INSTRUCTING AND ORGANIZING BUSINESS WITH PORTABLE MANUSCRIPTS

PAUL SCHWEITZER-MARTIN

MODERN-DAY COMPANIES AND stock markets heavily rely on a steady flow of information: elections, the weather, wars, and a broad range of political developments are monitored closely and immediately impact economic developments and growth predictions. Despite printed newspapers becoming fewer and less important in this day and age, the availability of information is abundant. News and especially data remain crucial and of significant value for modern societies and businesses. In the late Middle Ages, in a time before the modern concept of newspapers was common, news and data regarding prices or current developments were just as important. In recent publications, scholars such as Petra Schulte and Tobias Daniels have underscored the significance of information in late medieval societies.[1]

Especially regarding trade companies, Tobias Daniels argued that the trading company Große Ravensburger Handelsgesellschaft not only sold physical goods including linen, fustian, or sugar, but also traded in information as if it was a good in the fifteenth century.[2] This major institution was run by three family clans and their associates from southern Germany between around 1380 and 1530. The company's main office was set in Ravensburg about twenty-five kilometres north of Lake Constance. The headquarters' location provides the name used by scholars today despite it not being known as this in medieval sources. For instance, Spanish sources mention a *societas magna Alamanie* (large company from Germany), which seems to refer to what we know as Große Ravensburger Handelsgesellschaft. Scholars have pointed out that the description "large" probably was used to distinguish this specific group of merchants from other German trade corporations. Therefore, at least a second smaller trading company, if not multiple

1 Schulte, "Informationsverarbeitung"; Schulte, "Resilienz durch Information"; Daniels, "Vom Wert der Information"; for a broader perspective: Dover, *The Information Revolution*; for the sixteenth century: Bauer, *Zeitungen*.

2 Daniels, "Vom Wert der Information."

other companies, can be assumed. However, it is not clear when this second company might have existed and what relationship the two companies had.[3]

Besides the main office in Ravensburg, the group of merchants of which this company consisted also ran branches and warehouses in numerous places in central and southern Europe, many of them on the Iberian Peninsula.[4] While they sent paid messengers, family members, and their apprentices between the offices, one further means of communicating was to circulate lengthy newsletters, so called *Rekordanzen*,[5] between the different branches with a mix of economic and personal news. The term *Rekordanz* was used for these portable manuscripts by the trading company itself as can be seen in figure 2.5 below. These letters were each several pages long and written by hand.[6] So far mostly the economic content and not so much the materiality and mobility of these documents have been studied despite this communication being the backbone of an impressive economic network.[7] This chapter will analyze how the company's success, the associates' knowledge, and actions relied on the flow of information through these portable documents.

The Company and Previous Scholarship

In the late Middle Ages long distance trade was well established across Europe.[8] The Hanse discussed by Ulla Kypta and the trade company of the Fugger family probably are two of the best-known examples of successful long distance trading enterprises from the late Middle Ages and early modern period.[9] However, at the time, numerous companies were active. Some lesser known and also less studied examples are the Diesbach-Watt-Gesellschaft

3 Further names used in the sources for the company can also be found in Schulte, *Geschichte der grossen Ravensburger Handelsgesellschaft*, 1:44. For further discussions and varieties of the name see Falk, "Die Grosse Ravensburger Handelsgesellschaft," 98–108. She argues that there must have been companies from the Ravensburg area working simultaneously. See also Meyer, "Fernhandel mit Spanien im Spätmittelalter," 40.

4 Schulte, *Geschichte der grossen Ravensburger Handelsgesellschaft*, 1:98–103.

5 The term is related to the late medieval Italian *ricordanze*. For examples and the use of *ricordanze* by Italian merchants in the late Middle Ages see e.g., Jones, "Florentine Families"; Arlinghaus, *Zwischen Notiz und Bilanz*, 163–206.

6 Schulte, *Geschichte der grossen Ravensburger Handelsgesellschaft*, 1:112–18.

7 Schulte, *Geschichte der grossen Ravensburger Handelsgesellschaft*, 1:112–13.

8 Steinbach, *Einführung in die Wirtschaftsgeschichte*, 140–70.

9 On the Hanse see chap. 3 by Ulla Kypta in this volume; on the Fugger see Häberlein, *The Fuggers of Augsburg*.

from Switzerland, the Welser from Augsburg, the Imhof from Nürnberg, or the above mentioned Große Ravensburger Handelsgesellschaft.[10]

The latter company has been known for a long time and studied from the nineteenth century onwards especially by German historians.[11] Due to a fortunate coincidence numerous unknown sources regarding the business were found at the beginning of the twentieth century. This discovery multiplied the extant materials available to us and allowed for new insights. After the company had dissolved in 1530 one of its last bookkeepers, Alixius Hillson, held on to part of the records. After he had died, his grandson, a monk at the monastery in Salem, which is not far from Ravensburg, took these papers along with him for unknown reasons: maybe they functioned as some sort of family heirloom. At this point the documents vanish from the records. The monastery was secularized in 1803 and became state property. The documents were then recovered by an archivist more than a hundred years later in a drawer in the attic of the monastery. Supposedly birds had nested on the papers and they bore the label *unnütze Handelssachen* (useless trade papers).[12] Considering this transmission history, it is close to miraculous that the materials have survived.[13]

From the monastery in Salem the documents were taken to the state archive in Karlsruhe, at the time the capital of Baden. Today the archive is the Generallandesarchiv Karlsruhe, which is part of Baden-Württemberg's state archival system. The importance and value of the records became clear immediately at the archive and Aloys Schulte, a recognized economic historian, was asked to edit the documents.[14] Schulte was a history professor in Bonn at the time but had worked at the archive in Karlsruhe earlier in his career.[15] He prepared an edition of the papers which he published in 1923 together with two additional volumes of analysis.[16] Despite its age, to this day, this edition and study are the most important works of scholarship on the company's history and business practices. Besides the holdings in

---

10 Ammann, *Die Diesbach-Watt-Gesellschaft*; Rödel, "Imhof"; Häberlein and Burkhardt, *Die Welser*.

11 For an early study see Heyd, *Die Grosse Ravensburger Gesellschaft*.

12 Schulte, *Geschichte der grossen Ravensburger Handelsgesellschaft*, 1:2–3.

13 Even Arnold Esch points out this example in his essay, which remains important to this day, on transmission history. See Esch, "Überlieferungs-Chance und Überlieferungs-Zufall," 565.

14 Schulte, *Geschichte der grossen Ravensburger Handelsgesellschaft*, 1:3.

15 For Schulte's career see Braubach, "Aloys Schulte."

16 Schulte, *Geschichte der grossen Ravensburger Handelsgesellschaft*, 3 vols.

Karlsruhe, some documents referring to the Ravensburger Handelsgesellschaft can also be found in other archives.[17]

The company was founded in 1380 and dissolved for good in 1530.[18] It remains unknown precisely why the business ended at the time. Historians have explained this with reference to local conflicts, developments in global trade markets, and new investment strategies of the family members which focused more on the purchase of land around Ravensburg.[19] However, the exact circumstances are unlikely to be reconstructed. Likewise, no rules of procedure or statutes of the company survived; possibly they never existed at all.[20] Our knowledge on the company is therefore based mostly on business records, accounting information, and letters. It seems to have functioned such that every three years at a general meeting the company dissolved, distributed the income among its members, and immediately established itself anew with the members reinvesting their capital. Thus, the company only dissolved on paper, but the company's bookkeeping techniques of the time seem to have worked best this way. These general meetings took place in Ravensburg where the business and accounting papers were kept. From these documents it becomes clear that the company had a board consisting of nine members. These mostly were members of the three main families, the Humpis, the Mötteli, and Muntprat. Overall, all important positions were filled by family members and in-laws.[21]

Building mostly on Schulte's study there have been several publications in recent years.[22] Beate Falk, a retired archivist from Ravensburg, geared her studies mostly towards local readers interested in Ravensburg's history,

---

17 Schulte, *Geschichte der grossen Ravensburger Handelsgesellschaft*, 3:474–532; Heyd, *Die Grosse Ravensburger Gesellschaft*, 49–86.

18 Schulte, *Geschichte der grossen Ravensburger Handelsgesellschaft*, 1:17; 2:224.

19 Schulte, *Geschichte der grossen Ravensburger Handelsgesellschaft*, 2:224–42; Eitel, "Oberschwäbischer 'Welthandel,'" 74–76; Heyd, *Die Grosse Ravensburger Gesellschaft*, 43–46.

20 Schulte, *Geschichte der grossen Ravensburger Handelsgesellschaft*, 1:42. On the company's legal structure see Rehme, "Das rechtliche Wesen der großen Ravensburger Handelsgesellschaft"; see also Meyer, "Fernhandel mit Spanien im Spätmittelalter," 40–45.

21 A list of members can be found in Schulte, *Geschichte der grossen Ravensburger Handelsgesellschaft*, 1:148–208. For family structures and intermarriage see Meyer, "Die Große Ravensburger Handelsgesellschaft in der Region"; see also Eitel, "Die Teilhaber der Großen Ravensburger Handelsgesellschaft."

22 Schulte also published some shorter articles in addition to his edition. Schulte, "Die große Ravensburger Handelsgesellschaft und die Pflege der kirchlichen Kunst";

historical buildings in the city, and the company's significance for its vicinity and the region.[23] Others, like Andreas Meyer, engaged in questions of connectivity between Ravensburg and the regions the company traded with, e.g., Spain.[24] The flow of information has also been of interest to scholars as mentioned in the introduction of this chapter.[25] A brief summary of the company's activities and history can be found in the *Lexikon des Mittelalters*[26] and a more elaborate outline of the business can be found in the slightly more current article by Peter Eitel from 1997.[27] Despite the good source base and Schulte's edition no extensive studies have been conducted in recent years. It is therefore useful to reassess the existing scholarship as a whole and review all archival documents. As a first step this chapter will analyze one set of documents from the Generallandesarchiv Karlsruhe that were edited by Schulte, namely seven so-called *Rekordanzen*, that form a coherent group as source base.

The *Rekordanzen*

The *Rekordanzen* of the Ravensburger Handelsgesellschaft were newsletters and circulated a mix of economic and personal news between the company's main office and the different branches. Economic news for instance referred to the increase in prices for certain items and sales.[28] Personal news often highlighted where members of the company were sent or who was posted as tutor. In addition, often little reminders to certain people were sent on how to behave or whom to ask for advice.[29] More examples will be highlighted and analyzed in the following sections of the chapter.

Schulte, "Von der großen Handelsgesellschaft zu Ravensburg"; Schulte, "Ein wichtiger Fund zur Handelsgeschichte."

23 Falk, "Die Grosse Ravensburger Handelsgesellschaft"; Falk, *Kaufmannskontore und Adelssitze*; Schelle, *Die Große Oberschwäbische Handelsgesellschaft*. Similar: Widmann, *Die Bodenseehanse*; Eitel, "Oberschwäbischer 'Welthandel.'"

24 Meyer, "Fernhandel mit Spanien im Spätmittelalter"; Meyer, "Die Ravensburger Humpis-Gesellschaft"; Meyer, "Die Große Ravensburger Handelsgesellschaft in der Region"; Binder, "Vom frühesten Buchdruck in Spanien"; Müller, "Ein Schiffsraub im Mittelmeer."

25 Daniels, "Vom Wert der Information."

26 Schuler, "Ravensburger Handelsgesellschaft."

27 Eitel, "Oberschwäbischer 'Welthandel.'"

28 Schulte, *Geschichte der grossen Ravensburger Handelsgesellschaft*, 3:103, no. 8.

29 Schulte, *Geschichte der grossen Ravensburger Handelsgesellschaft*, 3:69, 77, 84, nos. 6–7.

Table 2.1. Overview of the seven *Rekordanzen* sent to and from Ravensburg between 1477 and 1480.

Date	State of transmission	Watermark	Document and page nos. from Schulte, *Geschichte*, vol. 3	Shelf mark Karlsruhe Generallandesarchiv	Place(s) of origin in alphabetical order	Location of recipient(s) in alphabetical order
Oct. 23, 1477	original	bull's head	no. 6, pp. 52–71	67 Nr. 1686, 10 (fols. 141–179)	Ravensburg	Avignon, Barcelona, Saragossa, Geneva, Lyon, Valencia
March 1478	original	bull's head	no. 7, pp. 71–97	67 Nr. 1684, 3 (fols. 20–56)	Ravensburg	Avignon, Barcelona, Saragossa, Geneva, Lyon, Valencia
June 25 to Aug. 10, 1479	original	scissors	no. 8, pp. 97–127	67 Nr. 1684, 14–18 (fols. 217–260)	Geneva, Lyon, Saragossa, Valencia	Ravensburg
Oct. 9, 1479	cartulary copy	bull's head	no. 9, pp. 127–56	67 Nr. 1684, 13 (fols. 172–216)	Ravensburg	Avignon, Barcelona, Saragossa, Lyon, Valencia
Apr. 4, 1480	original	hand with a star	no. 10, pp. 156–66	67 Nr. 1685, 2 (fols. 25–51)	Saragossa	Ravensburg
Aug. 29 to early Sept. 1480	cartulary copy	bull's head	no. 11, pp. 166–83	67 Nr. 1685, 3 (fols. 52–82)	Ravensburg	Avignon, Catalonia, Saragossa, Lyon, Valencia
Aug. 29 to Oct. 11, 1480	original	scissors with star	no. 12, pp. 183–94	67 Nr. 1685 (fols. 99–127)	Barcelona, Saragossa, Valencia	Ravensburg

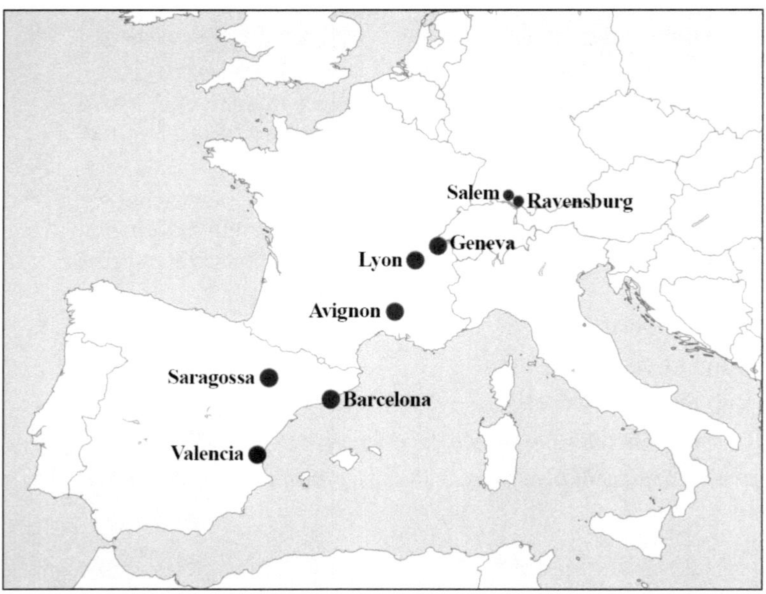

Figure 2.1. Map of recipients of *Rekordanzen*. Created by Johanna Eger based on https://commons.wikimedia.org/wiki/File:Europe_blank_laea_location_map.svg. Used with permission.

Such letters probably were very typical for merchant companies at the time but rarely have survived.[30] Aloys Schulte edited a total of seven *Rekordanzen* from the years 1477 to 1480.[31] (See table 2.1 for an overview.) All are kept at the Generallandesarchiv Karlsruhe today. In part, those that were sent from Ravensburg to the branches survive only as contemporary cartularies. The incoming letters sent to Ravensburg were transmitted as originals. All documents, both those surviving as originals and the cartularies are bound into books and are kept with the other above-mentioned documents from the monastery in Salem.[32] In total, the eight archival units regarding the Ravensburger Handelsgesellschaft contain more than 1,800 leaves of paper, most of which are tightly packed with text and accounting information both on the front and back of the sheets.

Schulte's edition made a substantial quantity of the documents from this collection accessible but not all of them, which is no surprise considering the vast number of documents and quantity of text. However, many of the pages that were not edited are barely legible due to handwriting and more often also due to damage through water or other wear (see figs. 2.2a and 2.2b). Each of the archival units is bound into a book. Within each of the eight volumes there are groups of documents, in the case of the *Rekordanzen* these often are made of one quire. The documents seem to be in the original medieval condition as they were stored by the company. Most subunits have a title page with a short description in a medieval hand and sometimes also bear the company's emblem (see fig. 2.3).[33] In his edition Schulte uses these short descriptions as introductions to the respective documents, e.g., as in the case of figure 2.5.

The fact that the books in part are cartularies means that they contain contemporary copies of documents which either were drafted or received by the main office in Ravensburg. An example of such a copy can be found

---

30 For similar documents from the late Middle Ages and early modern period see Jones, "Florentine Families"; Arlinghaus, *Zwischen Notiz und Bilanz*; Bauer, *Zeitungen*.

31 Schulte, *Geschichte der grossen Ravensburger Handelsgesellschaft*, 3:52–194, nos. 6–12.

32 The documents from the Ravensburger Handelsgesellschaft can be found at the Generallandesarchiv Karlsruhe under the following call numbers: 67 Nr. 1683–1689a. All documents are available as microfilm reproductions and can be viewed on site. The *Rekordanzen* can be found on the following pages of the documents: 67 Nr. 1684, 3 (fols. 20–56); 67 Nr. 1684, 13 (fols. 172–216); 67 Nr. 1684, 14–18 (fols. 217–260); 67 Nr. 1685, 2 (fols. 25–51); 67 Nr. 1685, 3 (fols. 52–82); 67 Nr. 1685 (fols. 99–127); 67 Nr. 1686, 10 (fols. 141–179).

33 For the company's emblem see Schulte, *Geschichte der grossen Ravensburger Handelsgesellschaft*, 1:44–46.

Figure 2.2a. A damaged page of the papers of the Ravensburger Handelsgesellschaft as microfilm reproduction. The label on the left-hand page indicates that the document is damaged. Karlsruhe, Generallandesarchiv (GLA), 67 Nr. 1689, fol. 26.

Figure 2.2b. Original of the damaged page in figure 2.2a. Karlsruhe, GLA, 67 Nr. 1689, fol. 26. All rights reserved by Karlsruhe, GLA. Used with permission.

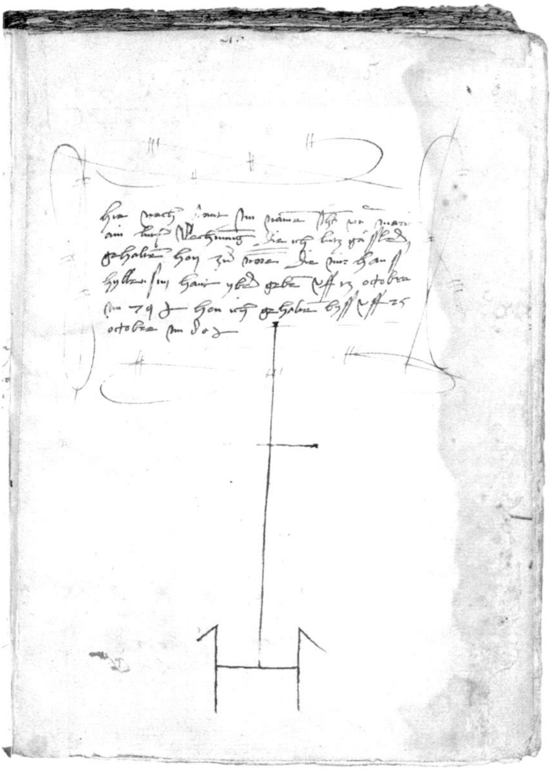

Figure 2.3. A title page of a document with a short description and the company's emblem. Karlsruhe, GLA, 67 Nr. 1688, fol. 5. All rights reserved by Karlsruhe, GLA. Used with permission.

in figure 2.4. These circumstances limit which aspects of materiality can be studied in those cases. Both the cartularies and the original *Rekordanzen* sent from and to Ravensburg are written on paper and were studied on microfilm at the archive in Karlsruhe. (See fig. 2.2a for an idea of the microfilm quality and appearance.) Figures 2.2–2.5 give a good impression of the documents that overall are very uniform. Most pages contain around twenty-seven lines of text.

According to Schulte's edition, a variety of watermarks are visible, indicating that a variety of paper stocks were used, despite the short period of only four years in which these *Rekordanzen* were compiled (see table 2.1).[34] The dominance of a bull's head watermark does not come as a surprise. This mark was used by paper mills in Ravensburg and it would make sense for

34 Schulte, *Geschichte der grossen Ravensburger Handelsgesellschaft*, 3:52, 97, 127, 156, 166, 183. The watermarks were not visible in the microfilm reproduction and thus could not be verified. Due to the poor condition of the documents the original could not be studied first-hand. I am all the more grateful that the archive in Karlsruhe could provide a few images of the original. Schulte's edition, however, is generally accepted to be accurate.

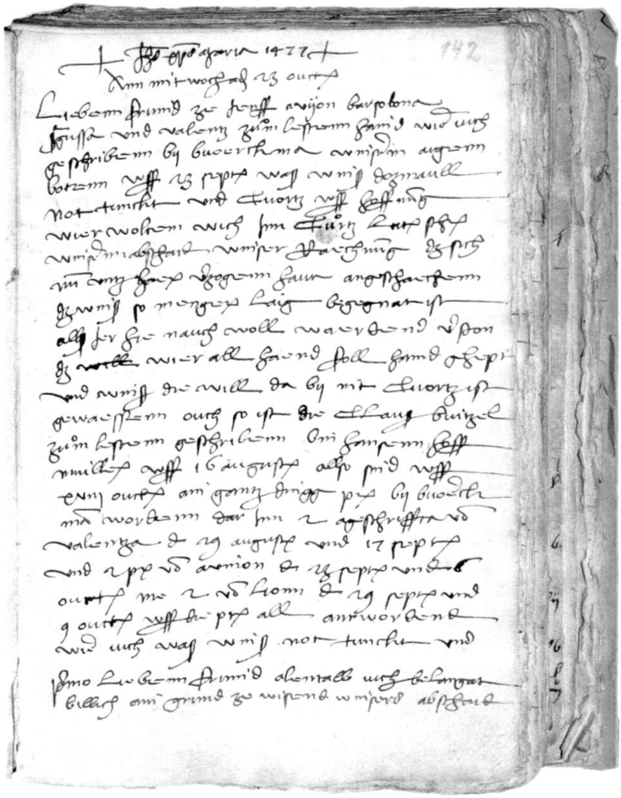

Figure 2.4. First page of a *Rekordanz* (cartulary copy) sent from Ravensburg to Geneva, Avignon, Barcelona, Saragossa, Valencia, and Lyon in October 1477. Date and addresses are indicated in the first lines. Karlsruhe, GLA, 67 Nr. 1686, fol. 141. All rights reserved by Karlsruhe, GLA. Used with permission.

Figure 2.5. Cover (dust wrapper) of an original *Rekordanz* (*Rekordantz fuir Rudolff per Raffenspurg*). Karlsruhe, GLA, 67 Nr. 1684, 14–18, fol. 217. All rights reserved by Karlsruhe, GLA. Used with permission.

the company to use local supplies.[35] Without analyzing the original documents this is not verifiable, since other mills also used this mark.[36] Of note here is the fact that in 1475 the Ravensburger Handelsgesellschaft ordered paper from Milan while it exported locally produced paper from Ravensburg to Würzburg in the same year.[37] Interestingly, those collections of letters sent from Ravensburg were all written on bull's head paper despite the fact that other types of paper seem to have also been available. This indicates that the merchants deliberately chose the local paper for their communications. This might have to do with the price, good availability, or also local pride. The incoming letters were all written on other paper stocks which suggests that the merchants did not take their writing paper with them from Ravensburg but probably acquired it on the road.[38]

Of the seven *Rekordanzen* edited by Schulte (see table 2.1) each are a collection of multiple shorter letters. Those coming from Ravensburg contain a first part addressed to all branches and then passages addressed to specific offices or members of the company. Those sent to Ravensburg are more like business reports from the branch offices to the headquarters. However, what is especially interesting about them is that they usually do not just contain news and information from one place but are collective letters with passages from different offices.[39] As context, it is important to emphasize that the *Rekordanzen* were not the only letters sent by and within the company, many more are in the archives or known from registries.[40] Also, some shorter documents were labelled as *Rekordanzen*.[41]

The company relied on a highly sophisticated system of messengers to exchange information between the branches and the main office. They sent both their own messengers and paid couriers.[42] The *Rekordanzen* are distinctive in the sense that they are extensive letter collections with multiple

---

35 Schultz, *Papierherstellung*. An English summary can be found in Meyer-Schlenkrich and Schweitzer-Martin, "How Does a New Trade Rise?"

36 Piccard, *Die Ochsenkopfwasserzeichen*.

37 Schulte, *Geschichte der grossen Ravensburger Handelsgesellschaft*, 2:221; See also Irsigler, "Papierhandel in Mitteleuropa," 318.

38 Schulte, *Geschichte der grossen Ravensburger Handelsgesellschaft*, 3:97, 156, 183.

39 Schulte, *Geschichte der grossen Ravensburger Handelsgesellschaft*, 1:112–13.

40 Schulte, *Geschichte der grossen Ravensburger Handelsgesellschaft*, 1:113.

41 E.g., Schulte, *Geschichte der grossen Ravensburger Handelsgesellschaft*, vol. 3, nos. 41, 42, 44, 47, 49, 50, 75.

42 Schulte, *Geschichte der grossen Ravensburger Handelsgesellschaft*, 1:112–18.

recipients in different locations or multiple authors and not just messages from one sender to one recipient. Table 2.1 and figure 2.1 break this down in more detail. One *Rekordanz* for instance (namely fig. 2.5) was sent to Avignon, Barcelona, Saragossa, Geneva, Lyon, and Valencia.[43] Aloys Schulte assumes that these letters were carried by members of the company and augmented by oral news.[44] The opening passage of another *Rekordanz* sent from Ravensburg in 1479 supports this assumption. It reads:

> Lieben frund zu Lyon, Awyon, Barsolon, Saragossa und Valenc. An ledsten hond wyer úch geschriben uff 15. passat big Burckman unssrem boten und sant úch dar mit brieff von F(rank)f(urt) und die loff, so sich disß vergangen meß zu F(rank)f(urt) hand verloffen. Sidert so ist únsß kain brieff von Valenc, Bar(solon), Saragosa nit worden, doch von Saragosa ist es nit seltza den ainr von Awyon di 6. passat ward únsß uff 21. passat und ainr von Lyon di 9. passat, sind únsß worden uff 21/25. passat. Dar uff wyer úch antwurtend was not. Dar zu so sol úch Jacob Rudolff unsser mainung muntlichen wol saga, dar zu sol sunst gluick dar in sin, so ist uch von alla dinga offt und dick gnug geschriben, aber unsß tonckt ir úber yllind unsß nit mit mit schriben, das unsß an ettlich nit gnu úbel kan verdriessen, felicht so wirt es der tag ainß besser, wilß yser fraw. Amen.
>
> (My dear friends in Lyon, Avignon, Barcelona, Saragossa, and Valencia. Last time I wrote to you on the 15th of the last month [i.e., September] and Bruckman, our messenger, brought our letter from Frankfurt and with it a report how business went at the last fair in Frankfurt. We received no letters since then from Valencia, Barcelona, or Saragossa. But we received one from Avignon from the 6th of the last month, that we received on the 21st and one from Lyon from the 9th that we received on the 21st/25th. These I want to answer as necessary. In addition, Jacob Rudolff should present our opinion orally. This approach might be more successful as we have already written about it often and clearly enough. We believe that you neglect us by not writing in return, which some of us find rather displeasing. But maybe one day things will be better, if Our Lady Mary wishes it. Amen.)[45]

There was no universal public postal service in the late Middle Ages. However, merchants, cities, and royal families are known to have established efficient means of communication by circulating letters, which enabled them to send

43 GLA Karlsruhe, 67 Nr. 1686, 10 (fols. 141–179); Schulte, *Geschichte der grossen Ravensburger Handelsgesellschaft*, 3:52–71, no. 6.

44 Schulte, *Geschichte der grossen Ravensburger Handelsgesellschaft*, 1:5–6, 122–23.

45 Schulte, *Geschichte der grossen Ravensburger Handelsgesellschaft*, 3:127, no. 9. (Translation provided by the author. It in part summarizes the German text, to make it more coherent for the reader.)

messages over long distances within a few days. Jürgen Herold, for example, studied letters sent in 1474/75 containing information regarding the siege of Neuss, a city close to Köln. At the time the siege was a topic at many royal courts and thus can be found in royal correspondence frequently. Herold found that messengers travelled with a speed of thirty and in some cases even up to sixty kilometres a day.[46] Besides for business reasons, letters at the time were used for political communication on the one hand and personal exchange on the other.[47] Oswald Bauer extensively studied the so-called *Fuggerzeitungen* (Fugger newspapers) of the sixteenth century.[48] While the content was in part similar to the *Rekordanzen*, the *Fuggerzeitungen* and also other newspapers of the sixteenth century clearly were addressed to a broader audience and also printed in some cases.[49]

Letters for the Ravensburger Handelsgesellschaft needed about nine days to travel to Lyon, twelve to Avignon, twenty-nine to Barcelona, or thirty-one to Valencia from Ravensburg.[50] Considering these more general findings on correspondence in the late Middle Ages, the blending of private and business information by the merchants of the Ravensburger Handelsgesellschaft was quite common. Also, the speed of delivery was not unusual for the time compared to the calculations Jürgen Herold made.[51]

On a more general level Mark Mersiowsky has emphasized how fruitful it is to analyze the materiality of such letters as this can help assess their transmission chances and how the documents were used.[52] As established in the introduction of this chapter most documents from the Ravensburger Handelsgesellschaft are only available to us today due the sheer luck of them being found by archivists and not being dumped after the monastery in Salem was secularized. This alone underscores the importance of reflecting on such questions. In terms of materiality and transmission Mersiowsky cites an interesting example from Bergen, a city on the western coast of Norway. Merchants there used thin wooden boards up until the fourteenth

---

46 Herold, "Report über Grenzen"; for the calculations see 142–43. More generally on messengers, see Folkens, "Städtische Gesandte"; on postal infrastructure, see Bauer, *Zeitungen*, 32–50.

47 Thaller, "Mechthild von der Pfalz und Margarethe von Savoyen."

48 Bauer, *Zeitungen*.

49 Bauer, *Zeitungen*, 31–42.

50 Schulte, *Geschichte der grossen Ravensburger Handelsgesellschaft*, 1:115. See 116 for more examples.

51 Herold, "Report über Grenzen," 142–43.

52 Mersiowsky, "Papyrus, Pergament, Papier."

century to communicate with their business partners. Later they seem to have switched to writing on paper, which unfortunately means these letters are lost for us today.[53] The specific layout or also cuts in parchment or paper that are unusual from today's perspective can often be explained by the sealing process of medieval documents. They were not sent in envelopes but folded such that the outer layer protected the inside of the document strongly influencing the documents' shape.[54]

Rekordanzen from Ravensburg

For the period from 1477 to 1480 every year a *Rekordanz* was sent from Ravensburg to the branch offices. Each of the four *Rekordanzen*, both the originals and the cartulary copies are on bull's head paper. The recipients varied slightly. The fact that all instructions and news items that were sent from Ravensburg to the branch offices were copied in cartularies before they were sent out on the road underscores this importance.

Each *Rekordanz* was sent to Avignon, Saragossa, Lyon, and Valencia. Only some were additionally sent to Barcelona, Catalonia, and Geneva. All four *Rekordanzen* have in common that they have multiple recipients and the general direction in which they were sent, namely to the southwest of Ravensburg. They thus open with greetings to the different branches. In 1477 Andreas Sattler writes "Liebenn fruind ze Jennff, Avyon, Barsolona, Saragussa und Valentz" (Dear friends in Geneva, Avignon, Barcelona, Saragossa, and Valencia) at the beginning of his letter.[55] Later on in the document he then specifically addresses only the office in Valencia by opening a paragraph with *Liebe Freunde zu Valentza* (Dear friends in Valencia).[56] Following this, one then finds advice (*Unser Rat ist*)[57] and specific instructions regarding what to buy and under which name to sell and buy goods.[58]

Often the instructions are very precise and quite elaborate:

> Chanamassari. Wir haben gehört, daß Ihr genug davon verkauft habt. Ist eine große Summe. Wir hoffen, daß das, was Ihr auf la Faerandina erhalten habt, auch meist verkauft sei. Kommt man mit der ersten Passage, daß man sie bleichen möchte, so verkaufte man statt 15 50 Ballen. Ihr zu Lyon: Laßt

53 Mersiowsky, "Papyrus, Pergament, Papier," 175–76.

54 Mersiowsky, "Papyrus, Pergament, Papier," 187–94.

55 Schulte, *Geschichte der grossen Ravensburger Handelsgesellschaft*, 3:52, no. 6.

56 Schulte, *Geschichte der grossen Ravensburger Handelsgesellschaft*, 3:58, no. 6.

57 Schulte, *Geschichte der grossen Ravensburger Handelsgesellschaft*, 3:67, no. 6.

58 Schulte, *Geschichte der grossen Ravensburger Handelsgesellschaft*, 3:68, no. 6.

von den Sorten kaufen, daran man am meisten hat: Buorc, 16^{e}, 13^{e}, Bellavilla, doch muß man die andern Sorten dabei haben. Es stände nicht übel, wenn Ihr von Valencia schriebet, an dieser Ware hätte man so viele Per cento, an der so viel. Ihr in Lyon braucht Fleiß für guten Kauf, will sie wohlfeil sein, so kauft desto mehr; teuer, desto minder. Früh im Jahr kommt man gut dazu. Nicht Jedermann kann Geld so lange darauf liegen lassen als wir, man muß sie "haimind," ehe andere darauf fallen. Wir hoffen: Ihr sollt aus Zucker, Seide Geld genug machen, doch das wird Hansen Lamparter lauter angeben.

(Chanamassari [most likely a kind of fabric]. We have heard that you have sold enough of it. It is a large sum. We hope that most of what you received at la Faerandina has also been sold. Once the first batch is ready to be bleached, we could sell 50 bales instead of 15. You at Lyon: Let them buy the varieties of which you have the most: Buorc, 16^{e}, 13^{e}, Bellavilla, but you must have the other varieties with you. It would not be a bad thing if you wrote from Valencia that they have so many percent of this product and so much of that. You in Lyon need diligence for a good purchase; if it is to be cheap, buy more; the more expensive, the less. Early in the year is a good time. Not everyone can leave money on it as long as we do, you have to "haimind" them before others fall on it. We hope so: You should make enough money out of sugar and silk, but Hansen Lamparter will say it the right way.)[59]

In some cases, like the *Rekordanz* from 1479, the authors also refer to information received in earlier letters or *Rekordanzen*. In the following example, Hans Hinderoffen's letter from Saragossa is mentioned and the amount of money that Hans Lamparter junior received as allowance on one of his business trips is discussed:

Item lieben frund. Hans Hinderoffen git an in siner r(ecordanz) von Saragossa, das er dem iungen Hansen Lamparter hab gen uff zerung, als er im gen Bilbau sant, 2 U jageses. Die schribt Polle in in nemen, ob sig nun Hansen Lamparter verrait haut ald nit, wys wyer nit, den Polle schribt sin zerung in uss gen, so er von Saragossa gen Barsolon thon haut.

(Dear friend. Hans Hinderoffen reports in his *Rekordanz* from Saragossa that he gave the young Hans Lamparter two pounds jageses when he sent him to Bilbao. These Polle writes in his name. Whether Hans Lamparter confused something or not, he does not know, because Polle writes his provisions ran out as he was departing from Saragossa to Barcelona.)[60]

---

59 Schulte, *Geschichte der grossen Ravensburger Handelsgesellschaft*, 3:58, no. 6. (Translation provided by the author.)

60 Schulte, *Geschichte der grossen Ravensburger Handelsgesellschaft*, 3:155, no. 9. (Translation provided by the author.) Another example can be found in Schulte, *Geschichte der grossen Ravensburger Handelsgesellschaft*, 3:191, 194, no. 12.

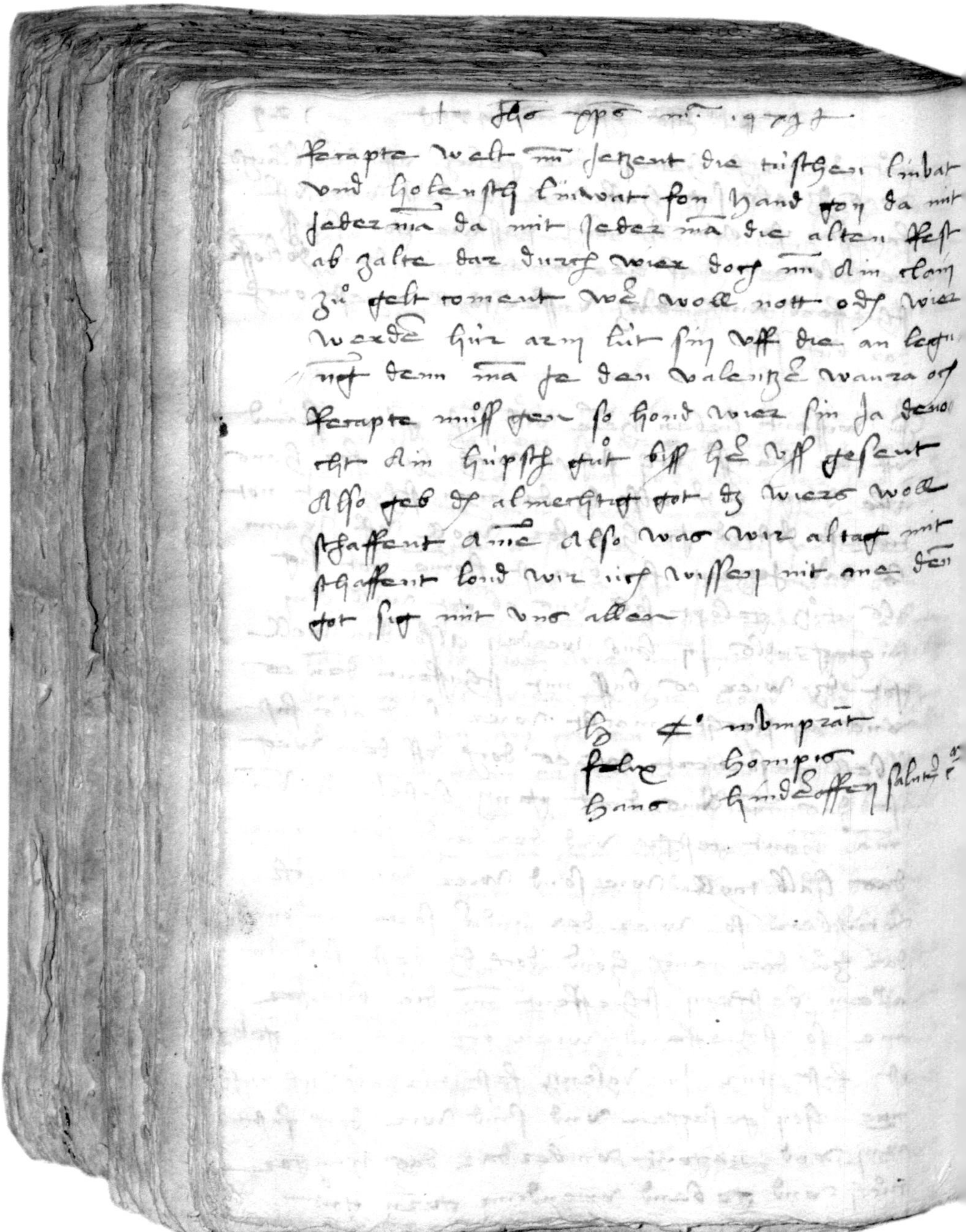

Figure 2.6. Pages from the *Rekordanz* sent to Ravensburg in 1479, carried by Jacob Rudolf. At the end of the left page one can read *H. C. Muprat, Felix Hompis and Hans Hinderoffen salute c(arissima)m.*

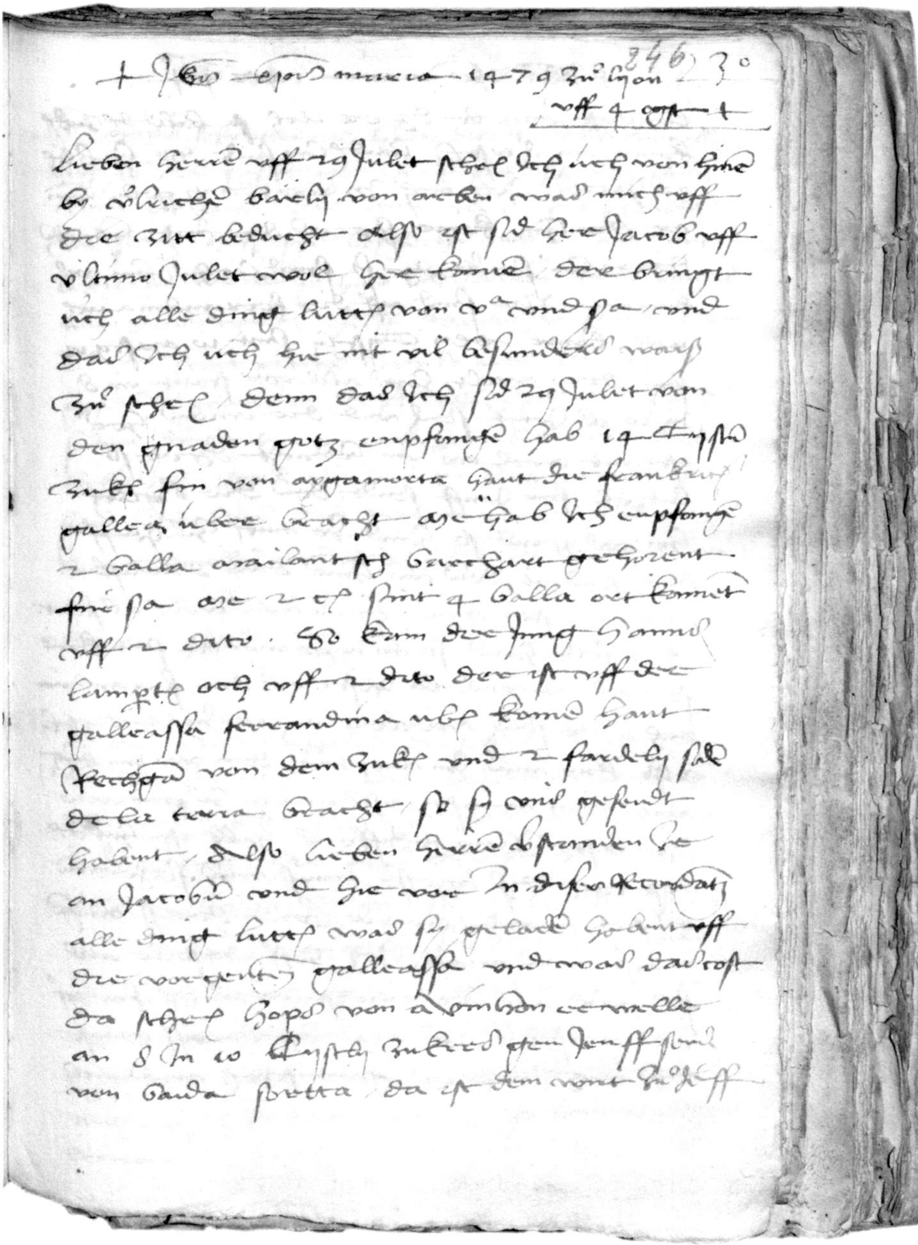

The right page opens with *†Ihs Xps Maria 1479 zu Lyon uff 4. ogst†*. Karlsruhe, GLA, 67 Nr. 1684, 14–18, fol. 246. All rights reserved by Karlsruhe, GLA. Used with permission.

These examples show that the office in Ravensburg knew precisely what was going on at the different branches, probably mostly due to incoming letters and messengers. They used this information and their experience in trade to instruct the younger family members and apprentices on how to do business on sight. They also encouraged the exchange of information between the different branches as the examples show. At the same time business and family news became closely intertwined.

The portability of these documents allowed for them to effectively disseminate news from the headquarters to the branches by both giving general and branch specific advice in the same letter. While it is not known how the *Rekordanzen* were presented to the individual branches, they helped to facilitate a coherent level of business knowledge within the company and seem to have been carried as one document from recipient to recipient. The communication within the company went in both directions as becomes apparent in table 2.1. In addition, instructions for the branch offices and also business reports became known to all members of the company in this way. The headquarters clearly managed the business affairs and let all members know of the instructions which might have increased mutual control far away from the board members in Ravensburg.

Rekordanzen to Ravensburg

While the *Rekordanzen* from Ravensburg were sent annually, the *Rekordanzen* from the branches to the headquarters vary much more in their length and seem not to have been sent at the same steady rate (although this might also be a false impression caused by the loss of documents or the company's filing practices). The fact that *Rekordanzen* both were sent from and to Ravensburg show that communication was not a one-way street within the trading company, or, in modern parlance "top down." The office in Ravensburg relied on receiving information from the branches, as demonstrated in the previous section, where instructions from Ravensburg are sent in response to certain developments.

While the four *Rekordanzen* from Ravensburg were quite uniform in many ways the documents sent to the headquarters vary. The three documents were each written on paper with a different watermark to name a primary difference in materiality, which is obviously a function of their different origins (see table 2.1). But in addition the authorship and design are different. While one letter is written by two merchants from

Saragossa,[61] a second one is sent from Valencia, Barcelona, and Saragossa jointly,[62] and a third one is sent from Geneva, Lyon, Saragossa, and Valencia with numerous different hands to be found in the document.[63] Franz-Josef Arlinghaus has pointed out that it was not unusual in the late Middle Ages to find multiple hands within one accounting or business document.[64] This third *Rekordanz* (see fig. 2.6) was carried by Jacob Rudolf and following the dates and signatures in the document, it seems to have been written and augmented along his journey: Valencia June 25th, Saragossa July 14th, Geneva August 10th.[65] In addition, a letter from Valencia from July 1st is added as copy. An example from this *Rekordanz* can be found in figure 2.6 where on the left-hand side a section of the report ends with the signatures of three merchants and the next page opens with the invocation of the Lady Mary. Most of the trade company's documents contain this invocation.

Carrying the *Rekordanz* from branch to branch had the advantage that the information sent to Ravensburg was made available to all branches along the way. This probably considerably sped up the dispersal of information, compared to the practice of first sending it to Ravensburg and then back to the branches. At the same time this method of having a messenger that carried a kind of notebook with continuous information or a "running list" might have been a good means of peer control.[66] All merchants along the way saw what the other branches had done in the previous weeks. And as all members of the company also seem to have been "shareholders" of the company it was important for all owners to be in control of their company. At the same time the *Rekordanzen* also kept the network up to date. These portable—and flexibly used—notebooks were thus a good means for both personal exchange and the control of company affairs, and as such, an explanation of why the Ravensburger Handelsgesellschaft used them to this extent.

---

61 Schulte, *Geschichte der grossen Ravensburger Handelsgesellschaft*, 3:156, no. 10.

62 Schulte, *Geschichte der grossen Ravensburger Handelsgesellschaft*, 3:183, no. 11.

63 Schulte, *Geschichte der grossen Ravensburger Handelsgesellschaft*, 3:97, no. 8.

64 Arlinghaus, "Account books," 48–49.

65 Schulte, *Geschichte der grossen Ravensburger Handelsgesellschaft*, 3:97, no. 8.

66 See chap. 1 above by Julia Bruch, in this volume, on peer control and keeping track of debts in account books as a comparable practice.

Conclusion

This chapter analyzed the so called *Rekordanzen* of the Ravensburger Handelsgesellschaft, which were an important means of communication and tool of control within the trading company. The family business heavily relied on sending messages to their branches and receiving information from them. Despite the flow of information being slower than today, the trading company tried to keep their members up to date and on the same level of information, in which the company seems to have succeeded in many cases. Both the *Rekordanzen* from Ravensburg to the branches and those sent back to the headquarters were carried by members of the company and not messengers. This facilitated not only the flow of information but personal contact between the merchants.

In many cases, the main office sent clear instructions to the branches, in other cases only advice or encouraged different branches to send each other specific information on trade developments. This emphasizes how well the headquarters were informed about the business situation abroad, even many hundred miles away. The backbone of this operation was the fast and steady flow of instructions and information. Letters between Ravensburg and the Iberian Peninsula needed only about a month. The *Rekordanzen* fostered a network and a community of merchants, that knew how business was going in the various locations, which apprentices were active in a specific location, and what deals were to be made. Since the Ravensburger Handelsgesellschaft was built on family ties, business news was almost always also family news. Sending astonishingly long letters that often consisted of multiple sheets of paper shows how important the flow of information was and how much time both senders and recipients invested into this stream of information and maybe also to control one another.

Bibliography

Manuscript and Archival Sources

Karlsruhe, Generallandesarchiv, 67 Nr. 1683 Berichte und Rechnungen von Angestellten der Großen Ravensburger Handelsgesellschaft, 1497–1508.

Karlsruhe, Generallandesarchiv, 67 Nr. 1684 Berichte und Rechnungen von Angestellten der Großen Ravensburger Handelsgesellschaft, 1478–1479.

Karlsruhe, Generallandesarchiv, 67 Nr. 1685 Berichte und Rechnungen von Angestellten der Großen Ravensburger Handelsgesellschaft, 1450–1515.

Karlsruhe, Generallandesarchiv, 67 Nr. 1686 Berichte und Rechnungen von Angestellten der Großen Ravensburger Handelsgesellschaft, 1474–1477.

Karlsruhe, Generallandesarchiv, 67 Nr. 1687 Berichte und Rechnungen von Angestellten der Großen Ravensburger Handelsgesellschaft, 1474–1479.

Karlsruhe, Generallandesarchiv, 67 Nr. 1688 Berichte und Rechnungen von Angestellten der Großen Ravensburger Handelsgesellschaft, 1472–1497.

Karlsruhe, Generallandesarchiv, 67 Nr. 1689 a Berichte und Rechnungen von Angestellten der Großen Ravensburger Handelsgesellschaft, 1477–1527.

Karlsruhe, Generallandesarchiv, 67 Nr. 1689 Berichte und Rechnungen von Angestellten der Großen Ravensburger Handelsgesellschaft, 1506–1526.

Printed Primary Sources

Schulte, Aloys. *Geschichte der grossen Ravensburger Handelsgesellschaft.* 3 vols. Deutsche Handelsakten des Mittelalters und der Neuzeit. Stuttgart: Deutsche Verlags-Anstalt, 1923.

Secondary Works

Ammann, Hektor. *Die Diesbach-Watt-Gesellschaft: Ein Beitrag zur Handelsgeschichte des 15. Jahrhunderts.* Mitteilungen zur vaterländischen Geschichte 37.1. St. Gallen: Fehr, 1928.

Arlinghaus, Franz-Josef. "Account Books." In *Transforming the Medieval World: Uses of Pragmatic Literacy in the Middle Ages.* Edited by Franz-Josef Arlinghaus et al., 43–69. Turnhout: Brepols 2006.

——. *Zwischen Notiz und Bilanz: Zur Eigendynamik des Schriftgebrauchs in der kaufmännischen Buchführung am Beispiel der Datini/di Berto-Handelsgesellschaft in Avignon (1367–1373).* Gesellschaft, Kultur und Schrift. Mediävistische Beiträge 8. Frankfurt am Main: Lang, 2000.

Bauer, Oswald. *Zeitungen vor der Zeitung: Die Fuggerzeitungen (1568–1605) und das frühmoderne Nachrichtensystem.* Colloquia Augustana 28. Berlin: Akademie, 2011.

Binder, Helmut. "Vom frühesten Buchdruck in Spanien: Die Große Ravensburger Handelsgesellschaft hatte Anteil an der Verbreitung von Gutenbergs Kunst." *Oberland* 11, no. 2 (2000): 34–42.

Braubach, Max. "Aloys Schulte und die rheinische Geschichte." *Rheinische Vierteljahrsblätter* 22 (1957): 1–30.

Daniels, Tobias. "Vom Wert der Information: Das Erdbeben von Neapel (1456) und die Beziehungen der Großen Ravensburger Handelsgesellschaft im Italien der Renaissance." *Vierteljahrschrift für Sozial- und Wirtschaftsgeschichte* 99 (2012): 43–64.

Dover, Paul. M. *The Information Revolution in Early Modern Europe*. New Approaches to European History 62. Cambridge: Cambridge University Press, 2021.

Eitel, Peter. "Oberschwäbischer 'Welthandel' im ausgehenden Mittelalter: Die Große Ravensburger Handelsgesellschaft." *Jahrbuch des Landkreises Lindau* 12 (1997): 63–76.

——. "Die Teilhaber der Großen Ravensburger Handelsgesellschaft (etwa 1400 bis 1530)." *Südwestdeutsche Blätter für Familien- und Wappenkunde* 16 (1979–1981): 507–8.

Esch, Arnold. "Überlieferungs-Chance und Überlieferungs-Zufall als methodisches Problem des Historikers." *Historische Zeitschrift* 240, no. 3 (1985): 529–70.

Falk, Beate. "Die 'Grosse Ravensburger Handelsgesellschaft' Entstehung, Folgen und Korrektur eines Geschichtsirrtums." *Schriften des Vereins für Geschichte des Bodensees und seiner Umgebung* 139 (2021): 95–111.

——. *Kaufmannskontore und Adelssitze: Die Humpishäuser in Ravensburg*. Vortrag zur Hauptversammlung der Museumsgesellschaft Ravensburg e.V. am 4. Mai 1996 in der Zehntscheuer Ravensburg: Überarbeitete Fassung. Ravensburg: Museumsgesellschaft, 1996.

Folkens, Christopher. "Städtische Gesandte als Akteure im Spannungsfeld zwischen Reichsstadt, Reich und Königtum: Das Beispiel des Frankfurter Gesandten Walter von Schwarzenberg." In *Kaiser, Reich und Reichsstadt in der Interaktion: 3. Tagung des Mühlhäuser Arbeitskreises für Reichsstadtgeschichte, Mühlhausen 16. bis 18. Februar 2015*. Edited by Thomas Lau and Helge Wittmann, 181–206. Petersberg: Imhof, 2016.

Häberlein, Mark. *The Fuggers of Augsburg: Pursuing Wealth and Honor in Renaissance Germany*. Charlottesville: University of Virginia Press, 2012.

Häberlein, Mark, and Johannes Burkhardt, eds. *Die Welser: Neue Forschungen zur Geschichte und Kultur des oberdeutschen Handelshauses*. Colloquia Augustana 16. Berlin: Akademie, 2002.

Herold, Jürgen. "Report über Grenzen: Die Berichte zum Neusser Krieg an den Hof der Gonzaga in Mantua (1474–1475): Nachrichtenbeschaffung und Nachrichtenübermittlung am Ende des Mittelalters." In *Briefe aus dem Spätmittelalter: Herrschaftliche Korrespondenz im deutschen Südwesten*. Edited by Peter Rückert, Nicole Bickhoff, and Mark Mersiowsky, 127–55. Stuttgart: Kohlhammer, 2015.

Heyd, Wilhelm. *Die Grosse Ravensburger Gesellschaft*. Beiträge zur Geschichte des deutschen Handels. Stuttgart: Cotta, 1890.

Irsigler, Franz. "Papierhandel in Mitteleuropa, 14.–16. Jahrhundert." In *Miscellanea Franz Irsigler: Festgabe zum 65. Geburtstag*. Edited by Volker Henn, Rudolf Holbach, Michel Pauly, and Wolfgang Schmid, 309–48. Trier: Porta Alba, 2006.

Jones, P. J. "Florentine Families and Florentine Diaries in the Fourteenth Century" *Papers of the British School at Rome* 24 (1956): 183–205.

Mersiowsky, Mark. "Papyrus, Pergament, Papier: Zur Materialität mittelalterlicher Briefe." In *Das Wasserzeichen-Informationssystem (WZIS): Bilanz und Perspektiven*. Edited by Erwin Frauenknecht, Gerald Maier, and Peter Rückert, 175–215. Stuttgart: Kohlhammer, 2017.

Meyer, Andreas. "Fernhandel mit Spanien im Spätmittelalter: Die Ravensburger Humpis-Gesellschaft." In *Oberschwaben und Spanien an der Schwelle zur Neuzeit: Einflüsse—Wirkungen—Beziehungen*. Edited by Dieter R. Bauer, Klaus Herbers, and Elmar L. Kuhn, 33–52. Ostfildern: Thorbecke, 2006.

——. "Die Große Ravensburger Handelsgesellschaft in der Region: Von der 'Bodenseehanse' zur Familiengesellschaft der Humpis." In *Kommunikation und Region.* Forum Suevicum: Beiträge zur Geschichte Ostschwabens und der benachbarten Regionen. Edited by Carl A. Hoffmann and Rolf Kießling, 249–304. Konstanz: UVK, 2001.

——. "Die Ravensburger Humpis-Gesellschaft und das Königreich Aragonien: Fernhandel im Spätmittelalter." In *Aragonien—Interkulturalität und Kompromiss.* Edited by Rafael Sevilla, Mario Kölling, and Rainer Öhlschläger, 198–208. Bad Honnef: Horlemann, 2008.

Meyer-Schlenkrich, Carla, and Paul Schweitzer-Martin. "How Does a New Trade Rise? The Case of Paper Production." In *Methods in Premodern Economic History: Case Studies from the Holy Roman Empire, c. 1300–c. 1600.* Edited by Julia Bruch, Ulla Kypta, and Tanja Skambraks, 225–28. Basingstoke: Palgrave Macmillan, 2019.

Müller, Karl Otto. "Ein Schiffsraub im Mittelmeer zum Nachteil der Großen Ravensburger Handelsgesellschaft (1490)." *Vierteljahrschrift für Sozial- und Wirtschaftsgeschichte* 26 (1933): 353–61.

Piccard, Gerhard. *Die Ochsenkopfwasserzeichen*, 3 vols. Die Wasserzeichenkartei Piccard im Hauptstaatsarchiv Stuttgart: Findbuch 2. Stuttgart: Kohlhammer, 1966.

Rehme, Paul. "Das rechtliche Wesen der großen Ravensburger Handelsgesellschaft." *Zeitschrift der Savigny-Stiftung für Rechtsgeschichte: Germanistische Abteilung* 47 (1927): 486–566.

Rödel, Dieter. "Imhof, Imhoff, Kaufmannsfamilie in Nürnberg." In *Lexikon des Mittelalters* 5 (1991): 385.

Schelle, Klaus. *Die Große Oberschwäbische Handelsgesellschaft.* Biberach: Biberacher, 2000.

Schuler, Peter-Johannes. "Ravensburger Handelsgesellschaft." In *Lexikon des Mittelalters* 7 (1995): 488–89.

Schulte, Aloys. "Die große Ravensburger Handelsgesellschaft und die Pflege der kirchlichen Kunst." *Archiv für Kulturgeschichte* 26 (1936): 73–88.

——. *Geschichte der grossen Ravensburger Handelsgesellschaft.* 3 vols. Deutsche Handelsakten des Mittelalters und der Neuzeit. Stuttgart: Deutsche Verlags-Anstalt, 1923.

——. "Von der großen Handelsgesellschaft zu Ravensburg, der größten deutschen Handelsfirma ihrer Zeit." *Das Bodenseebuch* 14 (1927): 22–28.

——. "Ein wichtiger Fund zur Handelsgeschichte." *Zeitschrift für die Geschichte des Oberrheins* 66, n.s. 27 (1912): 33–41.

Schulte, Petra. "Informationsverarbeitung in der Stadt des 12.–16. Jahrhunderts: Ein Resümee." In *Informationsverarbeitung in der Stadt des 12.–16. Jahrhunderts: Beiträge des interdisziplinären (Post-)Doc-Workshop des Trierer Zentrums für Mediävistik im November 2018.* Mittelalter: Interdisziplinäre Forschung und Rezeptionsgeschichte 2. Edited by Eric Burkart and Vincenz Schwab, 159–69.

——. "Resilienz durch Information: Einleitende Überlegungen." *Annales Mercaturae: Jahrbuch für internationale Handelsgeschichte / Yearbook for the History of International Trade and Commerce* 6 (2020): 7–18.

Schultz, Sandra. *Papierherstellung im deutschen Südwesten: Ein neues Gewerbe im späten Mittelalter.* Materiale Textkulturen 18. Berlin: De Gruyter, 2008.

Steinbach, Sebastian. *Einführung in die Wirtschaftsgeschichte.* vol. 3: *Mittelalter.* Stuttgart: Kohlhammer, 2021.

Thaller, Anja. "Mechthild von der Pfalz und Margarethe von Savoyen: zwei Fürstinnen im Spiegel ihrer Korrespondenz." In *Mechthild (1419–1482) im Spiegel der Zeit: Begleitbuch und Katalog zur Ausstellung des Landesarchivs Baden-Württemberg, Hauptstaatsarchiv Stuttgart*. Edited by Erwin Frauenknecht and Peter Rückert, 60–68. Stuttgart: Kohlhammer, 2019.

Widmann, Werner A. *Die Bodenseehanse: Aus der Geschichte der Großen Ravensburger Handelsgesellschaft*. München: Bayerische Vereinsbank, 1988.

Chapter 3

PORTABILITY FOR PARTICIPATION

ORGANIZING THE INTERESTS OF MERCHANT TOWNS AT HANSE DIETS

ULLA KYPTA

MERCHANTS DID NOT only organize their business activities, but also their political representation. One of the most prominent examples for a political organization of mercantile interests is the cooperation between various northern German towns, commonly known as "Hanse." From the middle of the fourteenth to the middle of the seventeenth century, representatives of the town councils met every few years at diets (or assemblies), to discuss matters of common policy. These diets relied on a number of documents that were exchanged between the various cities from Zeeland to Livland, from Westphalia to the towns at the shores of the Northern and Baltic Seas. The host town sent out invitations that were answered in different ways and typically sparked a surge of letters between the different towns to discuss travel arrangements and pre-meetings; delegates to the diets took with them instructions on how to vote and sent back reports of what was being discussed at the assembly; after a meeting was finished, the official minutes of the proceedings (the so called *Rezesse*) were dispatched from the host town's chancellery to the participating towns. Portable documents created a web of communication between Lübeck and the other Hanse towns as well as between the towns of the same region.

The assemblies of the towns in the northern Holy Roman Empire stand out from Europe's rich tradition of meeting cultures[1] because the Hanse diets were not structured hierarchically. Every town belonged to the same estate, so according to the premodern idea of the order of society no town was in a natural position to rule over another town at the diet. Of course, some towns could exercise more influence over others, especially Lübeck,

1 Blockmans, "A Typology of Representative Institutions in Late Medieval Europe"; for the German area, see Hardy, *Associative Political Culture in the Holy Roman Empire*; Hardy, "Tage (Courts, Councils and Diets)."

which emerged as a kind of head of Hanse cooperation.[2] However, neither Lübeck nor the diets as a whole could force a town to do anything.

The assemblies discussed numerous topics connected with their shared trading interests and reached a number of decisions, but they had no power of enforcement. Hanse cooperation could hence only succeed if the towns and merchants approved the decisions of the diets out of their own free will. It was therefore crucial that the diets were acknowledged as an authoritative body, even if their decisions were not legally binding. The diets had to be regarded as a legitimate organization.

This chapter discusses how the legitimacy of the Hanse diets was related to the portability of various documents connected to the assembly. Various documents carried between the different towns ensured the participation of the towns in all the proceedings from the planning of the diet to the distribution of the decision minutes. Participation in turn strengthened the legitimacy of the diets: they were regarded not as an entity that existed outside the towns, but rather as a common project of the towns.

In the following part of the chapter, I will shortly describe how Hanse cooperation came into being and how it functioned, and I will introduce the two diets of 1418 and 1518 that serve as my case studies. After I describe the materiality of the portable manuscripts, I analyse the participation of the towns in terms of the three stages before, during, and after the actual meeting. In each of the three stages, two types of documents can be distinguished according to who carried them where: (1a) documents carried before the Hanse diets from the inviting city (in these cases Lübeck) to the invited towns, (1b) documents carried before the Hanse diets between the invited towns, (2a) documents carried by the delegates from their hometown to the diet and vice versa, (2b) letters sent and received by the diet as an entity during the proceedings, (3a) minutes of the proceedings (*Rezesse*) sent to the town that had participated in the diet, (3b) *Rezesse* or extracts of them carried to the next diet as a source of information. For each group of documents, I will analyze the effect their portability had on the network of towns.

Hanse Diets, in Particular the Diets of 1418 and 1518

If merchants wanted to trade safely and successfully, they had to engage in political activities. Merchants needed political protection from rulers, for example the guarantee that they could travel through their territory without

2 Jenks, "A Capital Without a State."

being harmed. If possible, they tried to gain privileges from rulers such as the right to pay lower customs or to unload their ships on Sundays.[3] To gain a better bargaining position, merchants often joined forces with colleagues from their hometown who also traded at the same place. In rare cases, they cooperated with merchants from other towns as well. This was the case in the northern Holy Roman Empire. Merchants from Lübeck, Köln, Brunswick, Gdansk, and other cities often formed a community when they were doing business abroad. During the twelfth and thirteenth centuries, they gained trading privileges at Novgorod, London, Bruges, Bergen, and other smaller trading towns. The local ruler who issued the privileges termed them with a common denominator such as *Romani imperii mercatores*[4] (merchants of the Roman empire) or *mercatores regni Alemannie*[5] (merchants of the realm of Germany).

These privileges brought with them the need for further cooperation between the "imperial merchants" who were also called "Hanse merchants." The rights they had been granted had to be enforced in practice. Custom collectors, for instance, did not always acknowledge that Hanse merchants had to pay only the reduced fee.[6] With every accession of a new ruler, the privileges had to be renewed. Furthermore, the privileges were often connected with certain obligations on the part of the merchants. For example, the English king or queen insisted that they would not form trading companies with non-Hanse merchants, so that the privileges would only be used by Hanse merchants.[7] The merchants hence had to ensure that no-one endangered their privileges by ignoring these obligations. The merchant communities at Bruges, London, and other places organized themselves into *kontors* (branch offices) and elected elders as their governors.[8] The elders, however, could

3 See for Bruges Jenks, "Transaktionskostentheorie und die mittelalterliche Hanse."

4 Privilege issued by the count of Flanders in 1360, Höhlbaum, *Hansisches Urkundenbuch* 3, nos. 495, 243.

5 Privilege issued by the king of England in 1311; Böhmer and Techen, *Urkundenbuch der Stadt Lübeck*, vol. 1, nos. 419, 381.

6 This is one of the complaints the *kontor* of London brought forward to the diet of 1518, see *Hanserecesse* (hereafter HR) III, 7, no. 110, §1. (In citations of HR, the roman and Arabic numerals immediately following the abbreviation refer to series and volume numbers respectively. These items are listed in the Bibliography under HR by series and volume number.)

7 This royal concern is reported for instance in Gdansker Inventar, no. 15, 862 (1558).

8 On the *kontors* in general see Schubert, "Novgorod, Brügge, Bergen und London."

only discipline dangerous behaviour while the merchant in question was staying there. To make sure that everyone adhered to the rules, it was therefore necessary that the town councillors of the hometowns of the merchants also coordinated their actions. The town council of the respective hometown had the power to fine a merchant upon returning home. A network of towns was thus formed in order to govern the network of merchants.

During the fourteenth century, cooperation between the hometowns of the merchants became institutionalized as the Hanse diets.[9] Town councillors of various northern German towns met every few years to discuss matters of their common economic policy. Almost no aspect of their cooperation was formalized: the number of towns invited could vary from meeting to meeting, from more than thirty towns attending in 1418 to eight in 1449.[10] Meetings could be called whenever a town decided that important matters had to be discussed. However, the other towns had no obligation to come if they did not share this judgement. Meetings were presided over by the town councillors of the host town, which was in most cases but not always Lübeck. Resolutions were not immediately legally binding but had to be transferred into the law of the respective towns first.[11]

Only two basic rules seem to have been followed at each and every diet: during the debates, each town had to give its vote one after the other, and decisions had to be taken unanimously.[12] First, a topic was presented by the delegate of the presiding city, often Lübeck. Then, all the other delegates gave their votes, which means that they stated the position of their respective hometown in the matter. The order of discussion was fixed: the delegates sat in a kind of semi-circle, and each delegate was supposed to talk after the one sitting in front of him had finished his vote. After each round of votes, the presiding member tried to find a common position. If all delegates approved this common position, discussions on this topic were concluded. The common position was written down on the "*Rezess*," the minutes of the meetings (*recessus* literally means a law that has been "passed," but the *Rezesse* of the Hanse diets did not only mention the decisions of the diet, but also the discussions leading to a decision). In many cases, this consensus could consist

9 The term "Hanse" was used by the towns to denominate common projects from the middle of the fourteenth century onwards, see Behrmann, "Über Zeichen, Zeremoniell und Hansebegriff auf hansischen Tagfahrten."

10 For an analysis of the attendance see Huang, "Die *stede van der dudeschen hence*."

11 Henn, "Hansische Tagfahrten in der zweiten Hälfte des 14. Jahrhunderts," 8.

12 Hammel-Kiesow and Puhle, *Die Hanse*, 84.

in the notion that the delegates could not come to an agreement at the present moment and would discuss the issue further at future diets.

Despite their very informal structure, Hanse diets continued to take place for roughly three hundred years, from the middle of the fourteenth century until 1669, when after the Thirty Years' War only a few of the Hanse towns remained autonomous. Studying the manuscripts that travelled through Europe in connection with the Hanse diets helps to explain why.

In order to do that, I analyze the portability of the manuscripts for the two Hanse diets of 1418 and 1518. At the beginning of the fifteenth century, the meetings had established certain routine processes, so the Hanse diets can be regarded as fully formed from then on.[13] The last diet took place in 1669, however, the source edition only runs up to the meeting of 1534.[14] For the current chapter, the decision was taken to work with the source editions since the editors did not only include the minutes of the meetings, but also all the documents they considered as related to the meetings such as invitations, reports, and letters that were stored in the various archives of Hanse towns. This decision to include so many documents is open to question, but in this case it proves helpful because it enables me to study which documents were carried in connection with the diets in regard to their couriers, their origins, and their destinations.[15] I chose the diets of 1418 and 1518 as case studies because the one was an exceptional, the other a quite typical meeting: the Hanse diet of 1418 counts among the most famous diets in Hanse research since a large number of towns attended and agreed upon some important ideas to restructure their cooperation, most prominently they asked Lübeck to represent Hanse interests in the time between their meetings.[16] In 1518, by contrast, an average number of towns convened, it lasted for the usual length of time and discussed the typical recurrent topics.

---

13 See Huang, "Die *stede van der dudeschen hense*."

14 The editions have all been digitized and can be accessed via https://www.hansischergeschichtsverein.de/hanserecesse, accessed June 30, 2025. The newer minutes are currently being transcribed by a citizen science project; see https://fgho.eu/en/projects/hanse-quellen-lesen, accessed June 30, 2025.

15 Huang and Kypta, "Ein neues Haus auf altem Fundament"; Jahnke, "Die Reliquien jener grossartigen Bewegung"; Jahnke, "Die Recesse und andere Akten der Hansetage"; Jahnke, "Hansische Urkundenbuch."

16 Hammel-Kiesow and Puhle call it "the probably most important meeting in Hanse history"; Hammel-Kiesow and Puhle, *Die Hanse*, 88. For the role of Lübeck, see Jenks, "A Capital Without a State."

At the diet of 1418, delegates from a record number of thirty-five towns from various regions were present, namely (in the order of seating) Lübeck, Köln, Bremen, Rostock, Stralsund, Wismar, Brunswick, Gdansk, Wisby, Riga, Dorpat, Reval (Tallinn), Stettin, Anklam, Osnabrück, Stargard, Stade, Buxtehude, Salzwedel, Stendal, Hamburg, Dortmund, Lüneburg, Greifswald, Münster, Kolberg, Nijmegen, Deventer, Zutphen, Zwolle, Harderwijk, and Elburg. The *kontor* in Bruges was represented by an alderman. The Grand Master of the Teutonic Order had sent an envoy, as well as the archbishop of Bremen.[17] The meeting lasted from June 24, 1418, until August. The towns discussed the *Pfundgeld* (a custom the towns levied temporarily in emergency situations, for instance to finance wars), problems of the *kontor* in Bruges and Bergen, and dealings with the king of Denmark and the dukes of Mecklenburg and Schleswig. They tried to mediate various conflicts between their members, for example between Hamburg and Bremen or between Greifswald and Gdansk. Henry V of England had complained about merchants from Greifswald, a Danish captain about merchants from Reval. Furthermore, the towns restructured their internal organization by asking Lübeck to act in their collective name when no Hanse diet was being held. Since Lübeck and some other towns had to face internal conflicts in the years before the diet, the representatives underlined in the *Rezess* that the unchallenged regiment of the city council was a necessary prerequisite for participation in Hanse diets.

In 1518, the delegates of seventeen towns convened, namely Lübeck, Lüneburg, Hamburg, Rostock, Wismar, Köln, Dortmund, Minden, Magdeburg, Brunswick, Goslar, Hildesheim, Göttingen, Einbeck, Hannover, Gdansk, and Riga.[18] The *kontors* of Bruges, London, and Bergen had each sent the head of their administrative staff, their secretary. The diet began on June 19, 1518, and ended three and a half weeks later on July 14. As at most diets, the towns first discussed conflicts about the seating order, and they acknowledged various excuses from towns who did not send delegates. Second, as had also become routine during the last century, they heard the complaints of the *kontors*' secretaries and decided whether and how to handle these. Furthermore, as usual, they tried to solve various conflicts between Hanse towns, in this case between Lübeck and Gdansk, Gdansk and Hamburg, and Hamburg and Riga. Rostock complained about taxes in Denmark, Riga about problems with the quality of linen products. The towns reinforced a ban they

17 HR I, 6, nos. 556, 534–49.

18 HR III, 7, nos. 108, 142–87.

had issued many times before, namely the prohibition for any Hanse town to build ships for non-Hanse merchants.[19] They also discussed, as many times before, whether to form a more formal alliance, a so-called "tohopesate."

Materiality of the Portable Manuscripts

Before I go on to analyze in detail how the portability of various kinds of manuscripts enabled the cooperation of Hanse towns, it is important to get an impression of their material features. The Hanse documents differed with regard to their materiality, which influenced their portability. We can distinguish three classes of manuscripts: first, letters and reports (very small and informal, highly portable); second, invitations, instructions, and agendas (more formal, but still quite small, still easy to transport); and third, the protocols of the meetings (not very formal, but large and thick and so portable only to a certain degree).

First, as the rest of the chapter will show, letters—not surprisingly—played a crucial part in various stages of Hanse cooperation. In the introduction we already pointed out how letter writing became an important activity for merchants during the late Middle Ages, and the same is true for town councillors and delegates. The number of manuscripts written for everyday purposes significantly increased from the twelfth century onwards, and letters can be regarded as the most ubiquitous form of everyday writing. Letters between merchants and between town councils do not look very impressive, they are a far cry from charters, illuminated bibles or other splendid manuscripts the Middle Ages are renowned for. Letters were typically even smaller than the A4 format of today and the page was filled, leaving only a very small margin. Official letters from one town council to the other were usually issued with more care than merchants' correspondence, and they carried the seal of the sender. Only very few of the letters survived over the centuries, but towns often copied the content into the city books. The Hanse diets also inserted the text of letters they posted and received into the official protocol, the *Rezess* (see fig. 3.1). This is how we know that letters played such an important part in organizing urban life and trade in the late Middle Ages.

Letters were intended to be portable, so they were drawn up in a way that made them easily transportable: they were written on small sheets of parchment and later paper, folded, and locked by special folding and locking

19 For this discussion, see Jenks, "Zum hansischen Gästerecht."

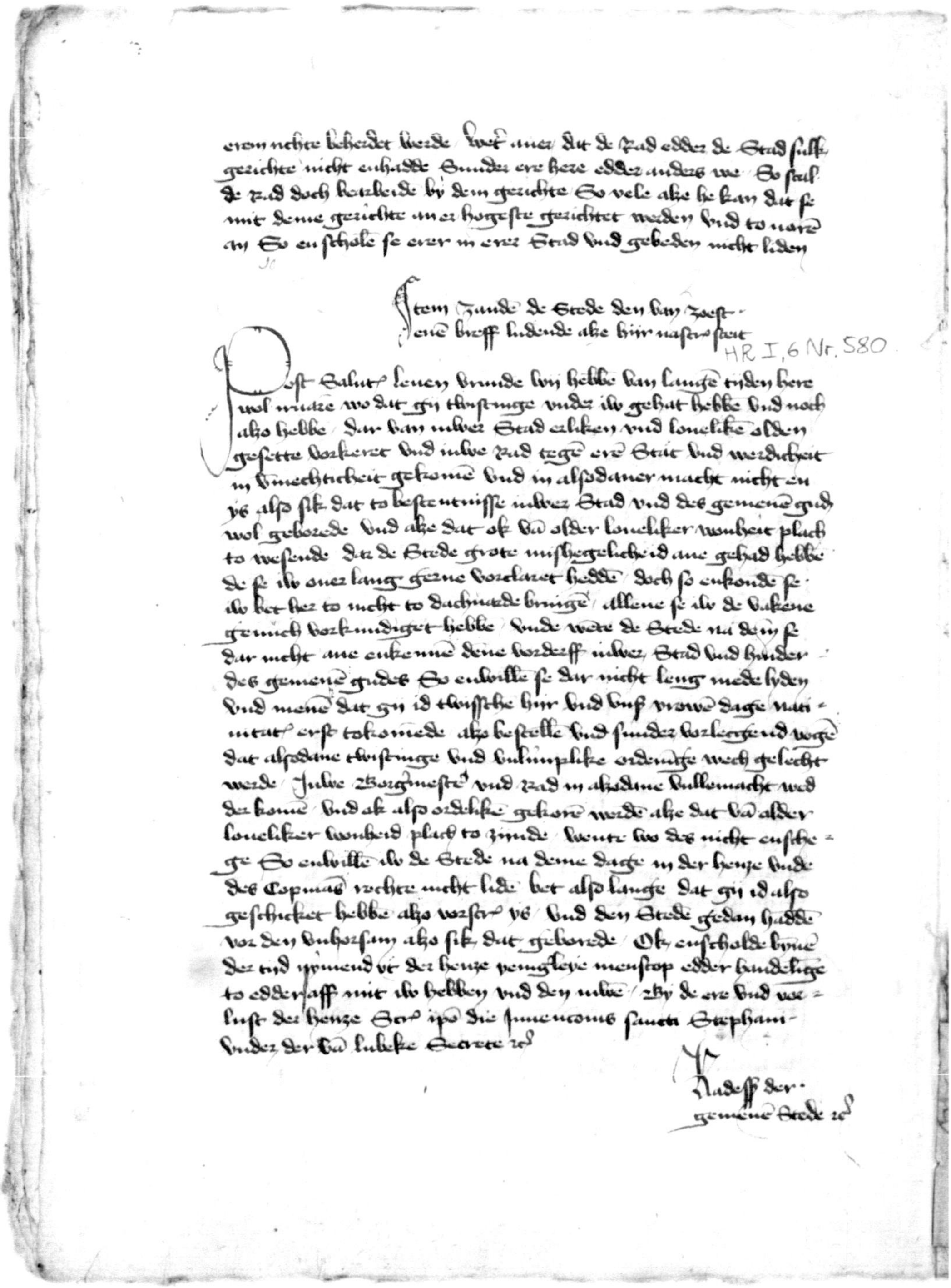

Figure 3.1. Letter from the diet in Lübeck to the town of Soest, inserted into the *Rezess*. Lübeck, Archiv der Hansestadt Lübeck, ASA Externa Hanseatica 19, fol. 18b. Used with permission.

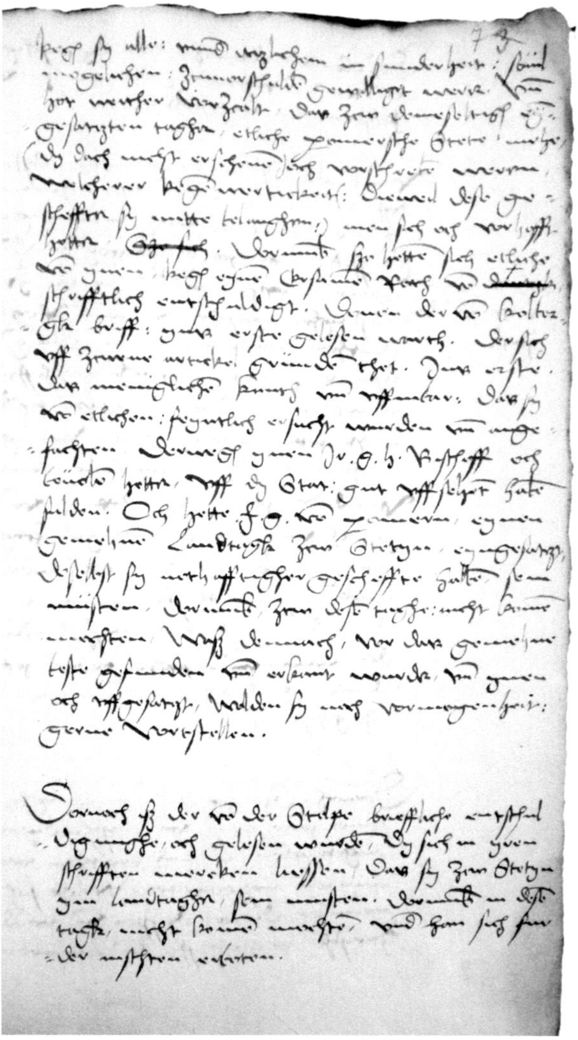

Figure 3.2. One page of the report by the delegates of Gdansk to the Gdansk city council. Gdansk, Archiwum Państwowe w Gdańsku, 300, 28, no. 5 (1523). Used with permission.

techniques.[20] Reports sent by the delegates to their hometowns resemble letters, and often came enclosed in accompanying letters. Like letters, they were written in a nonformal style and script, without much time and effort to design a certain layout. They had to be dispatched quickly in order to keep the town council abreast of developments at the diets. But they left some margin to add corrections and additions (see fig. 3.2).

Second, the invitations to a meeting, often including the agenda, and the instructions that delegates were given by their fellow councillors could be prepared with more care because time was generally less pressing. They were written on larger sheets, structured in clear paragraphs, with a large margin to make the document more solemn and official (see fig. 3.3). The agenda was subdivided in numbered items, and the instructions followed the items on the agenda: point after point, the town council gave its delegate directions how he was to vote regarding this item, whether he could be open for compromises or where he should draw a red line.

The instruction looked as formal as the agendas. They can be regarded as pragmatic writings in the sense that they served a certain administrative

20 These techniques are being researched by the "letterlocking" project, see https://letterlocking.org, accessed June 30, 2025.

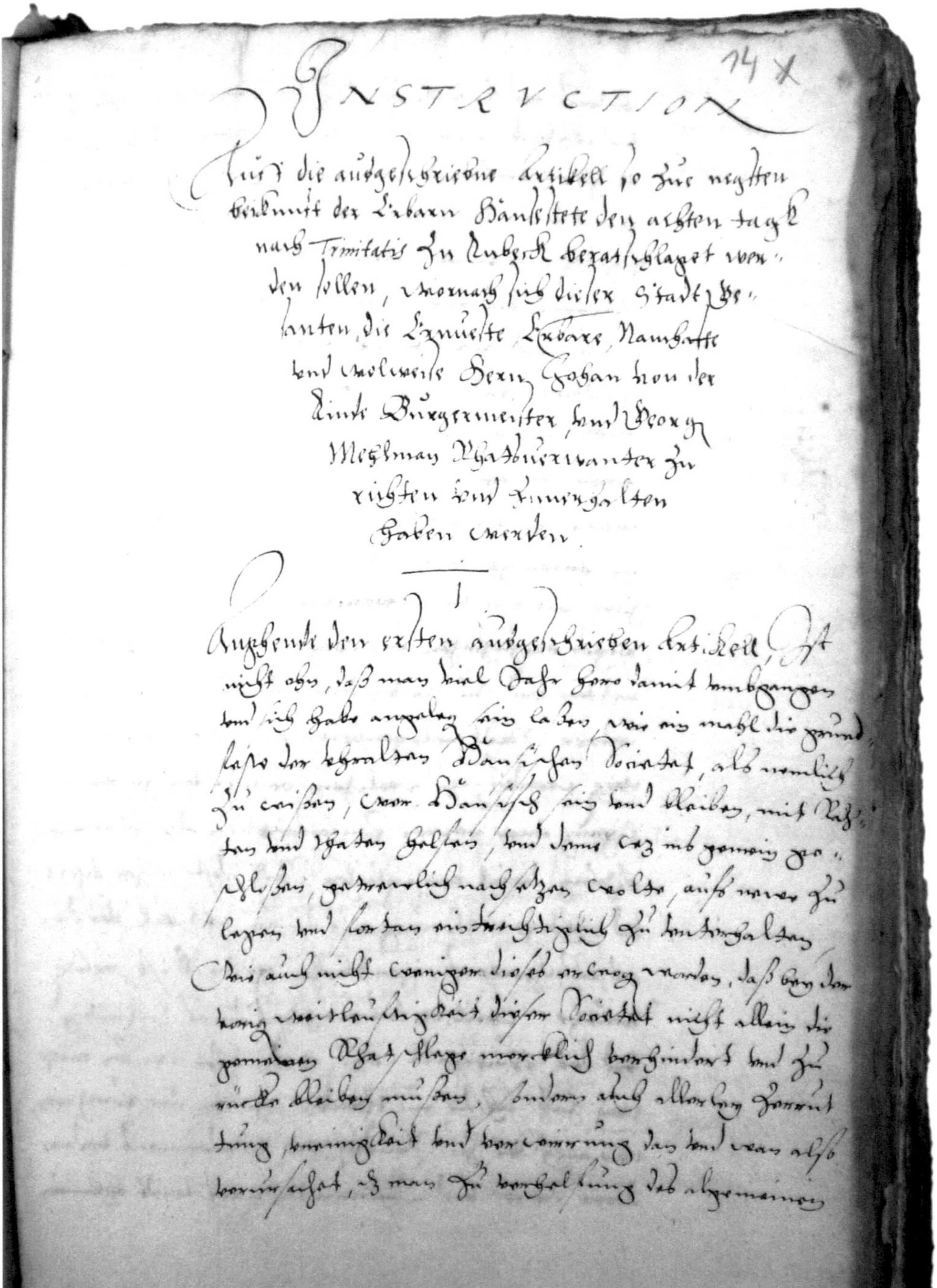

Figure 3.3. Instruction for the delegates from Gdansk to the diet in Lübeck, first page. Gdansk, Archiwum Państwowe w Gdańsku, 300, 28, no. 59 (1591). Used with permission.

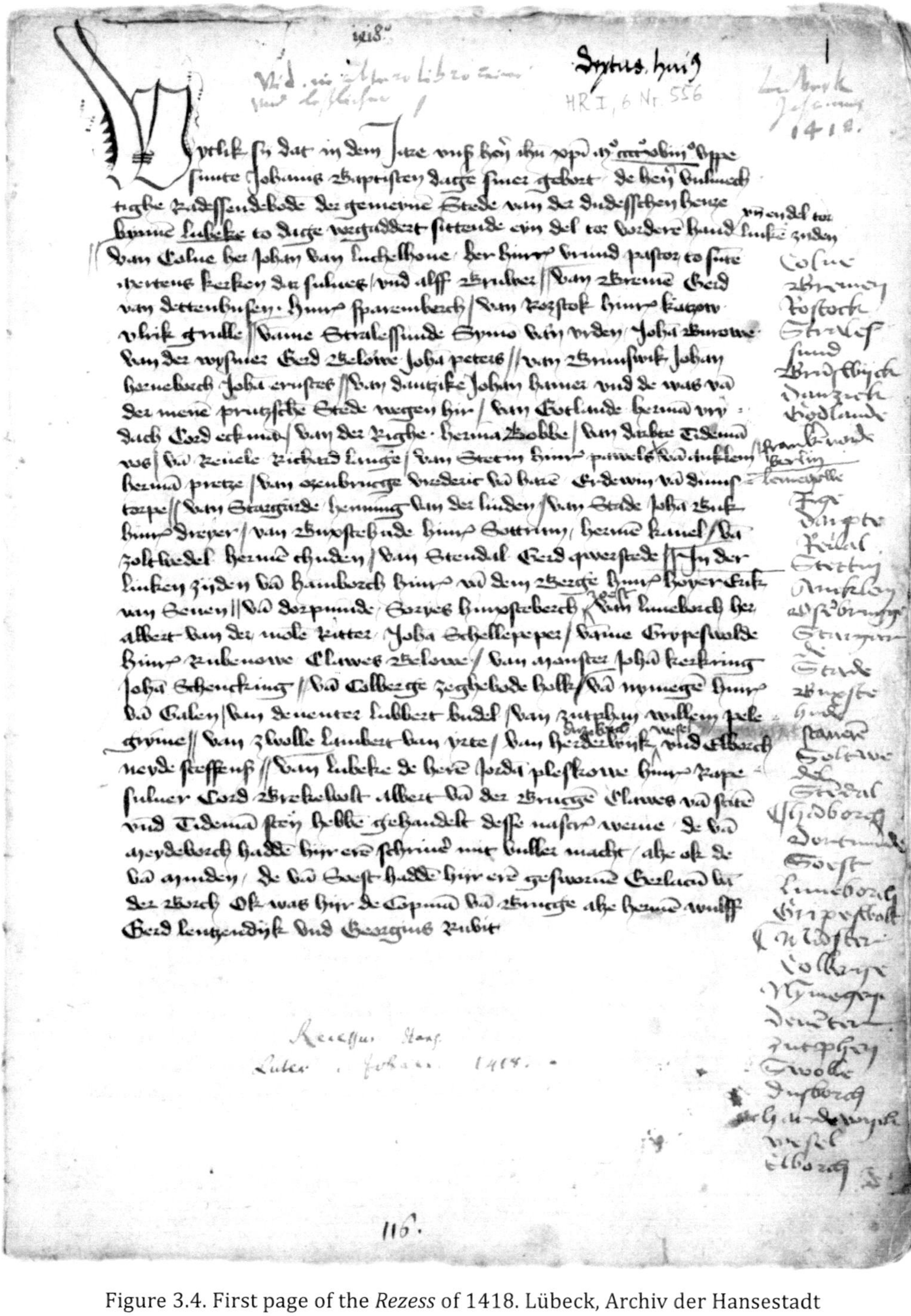

Figure 3.4. First page of the *Rezess* of 1418. Lübeck, Archiv der Hansestadt Lübeck, ASA Externa Hanseatica 19, fol. 1. Used with permission.

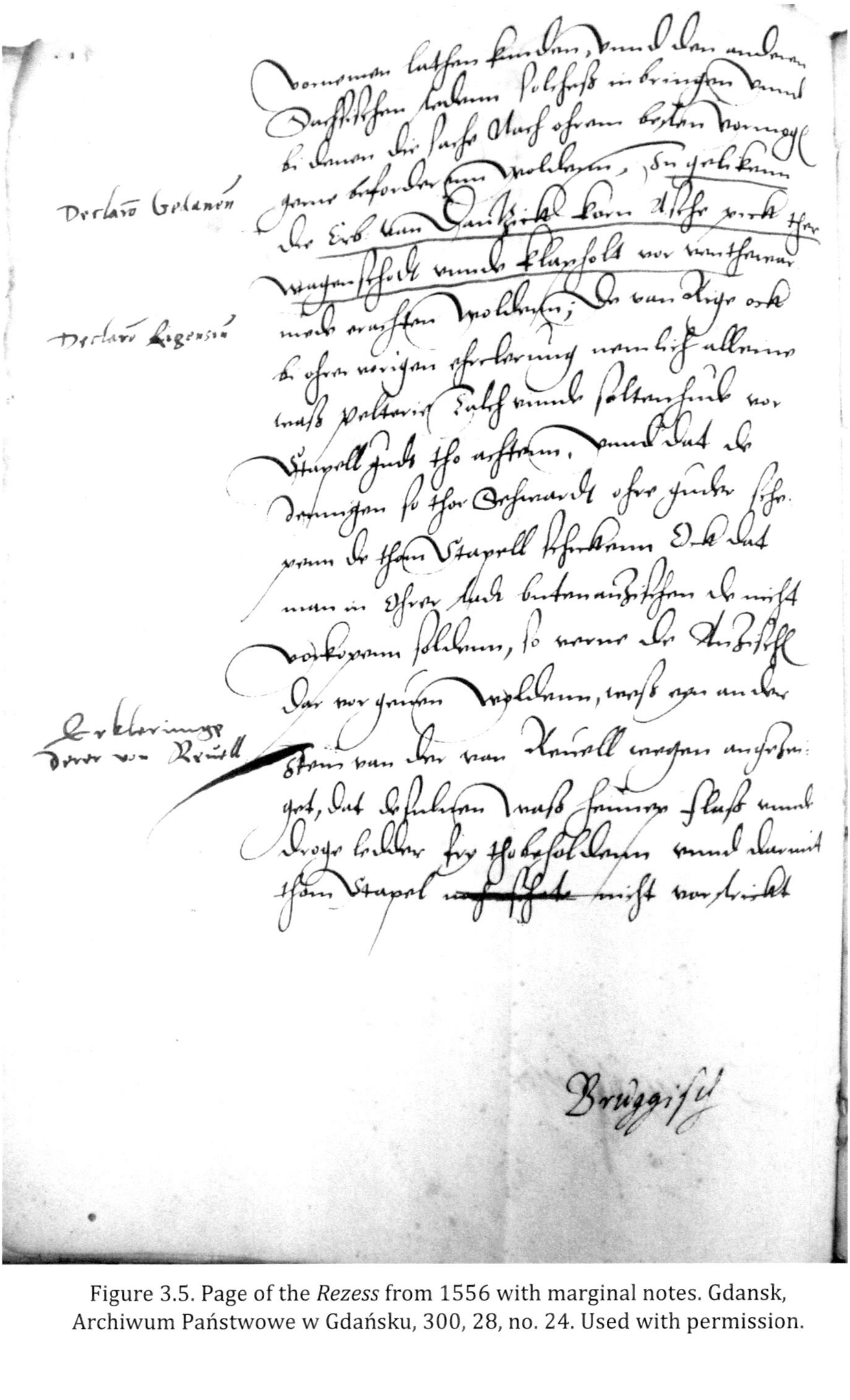

Figure 3.5. Page of the *Rezess* from 1556 with marginal notes. Gdansk, Archiwum Państwowe w Gdańsku, 300, 28, no. 24. Used with permission.

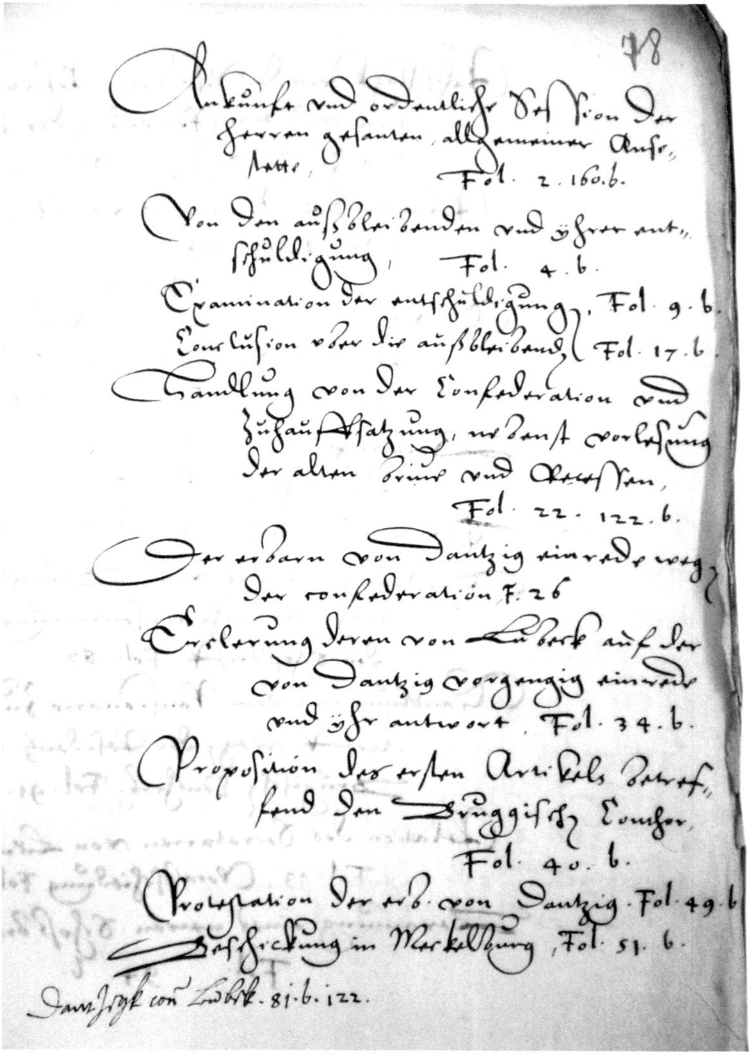

Figure 3.6a. Register at the end of the *Rezess* from 1540. Gdansk, Archiwum Państwowe w Gdańsku, 300, 28, no. 12, p. 1. Used with permission.

purpose, but the design of the manuscript was nevertheless intended to convey the authority of the issuing body. The invitations were meant to make it clear that the meeting of the Hanse towns was a solemn assembly that carried some authority; and the instructions were designed to underline that the town councils had the last say in all important matters, and that the town's delegate had to exact their positions.

Third, the course of the discussions and the decisions reached were written down in the *Rezesse* (see fig. 3.4). Even though they were intended to carry a lot of authority, they lack any grandiosity, they do not sport any illuminated initials, they were not bound in some precious material. This was

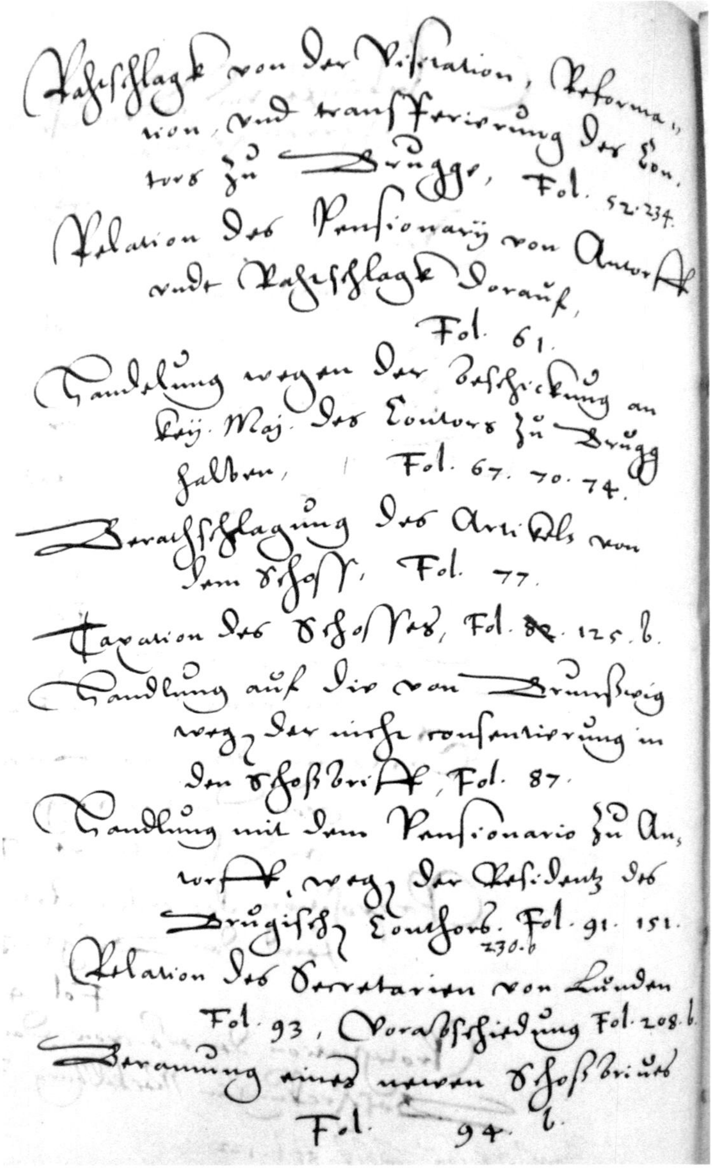
Rathschlagk von der Visitation, Reforma-
tion, und transferierung der Con-
tors zu Brugge, Fol. 52. 234.
Relation des Pensionarij von Antorff
undt Rathschlagk darauf,
Fol. 61.
Handlung wegen der beschickung an
Kay. Maj. des Contors zu Brugg
halben, Fol. 67. 70. 74.
Berathschlagung des Artickels von
dem Schoss. Fol. 77.
Taxation des Schosses, Fol. 125. b.
Handlung auf die von Braunschweig
wegen der nicht consentierung in
den Schoßbrieff, Fol. 87.
Handlung mit dem Pensionario zu An-
torff, wegen der Residentz des
Brugischen Contors. Fol. 91. 151. 230. b
Relation des Secretarien von Lunden
Fol. 93, Vorabscheidung Fol. 208. b
Beramung eines newen Schoßbrieffs
Fol. 94. b.

Figure 3.6b. Register at the end of the *Rezess* from 1540. Gdansk, Archiwum Państwowe w Gdańsku, 300, 28, no. 12, p. 2. Used with permission.

due to practical reasons: *Rezesse* were thick documents,[21] every town present at a diet received a copy, and diets occurred every few years. It would hence have cost too much time and effort to make them into magnificent manuscripts. What the manuscripts show, however, is that contemporaries

21 This is especially true of the *Rezesse* drafted in the sixteenth and early seventeenth centuries. For instance, the *Rezess* from 1549 consists of 367 pages, the one from 1611 of 247 pages. Archiwum Państwowe w Gdańsku, 300, 28, no. 14 and no. 78.

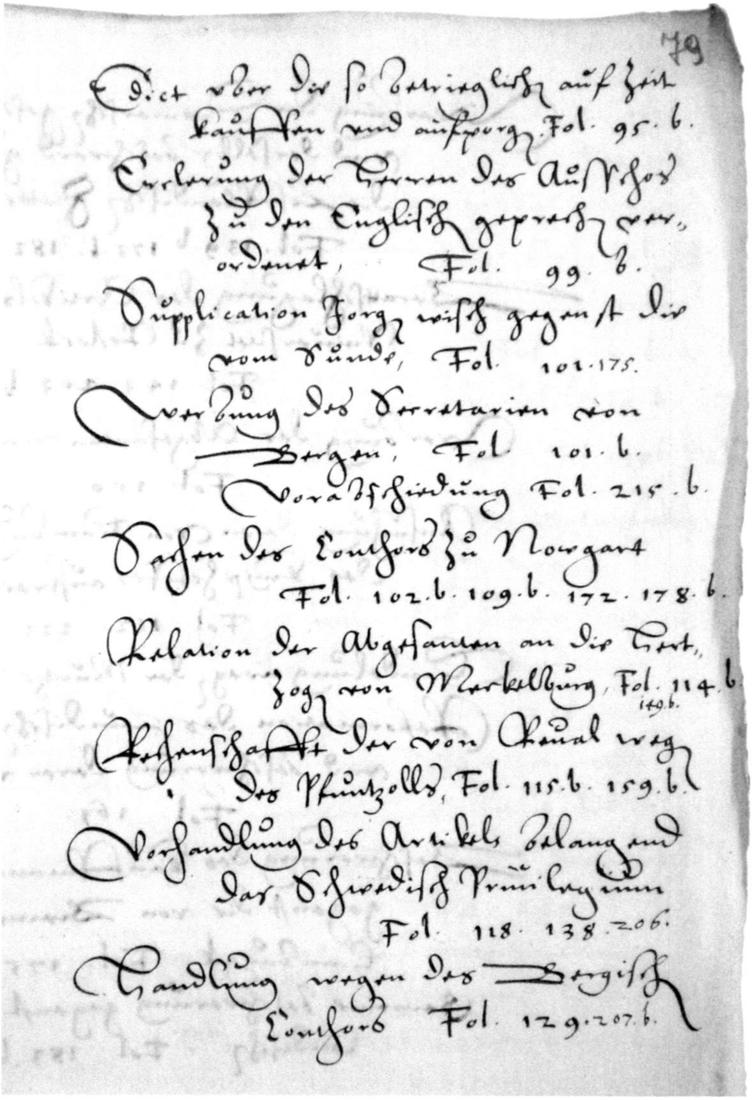

Figure 3.6c. Register at the end of the *Rezess* from 1540. Gdansk, Archiwum Państwowe w Gdańsku, 300, 28, no. 12, p. 3. Used with permission.

worked with them, they consulted the *Rezesse* for information. The manuscripts were set up with quite a margin of about a third of the page, and contemporaries wrote short notes in them to characterize the content. For example, the *Rezess* of 1554 was examined by someone who had an obvious interest in a discussion concerning the trading outpost in Bruges. He wrote the following statement in the margin of the page on which this discussion was recorded: "declaration by Gdansk, declaration by Riga, declarations by the delegates from Tallin" (see fig. 3.5). In some manuscripts, a register helps to find the topics of discussion (see fig. 3.6a–f).

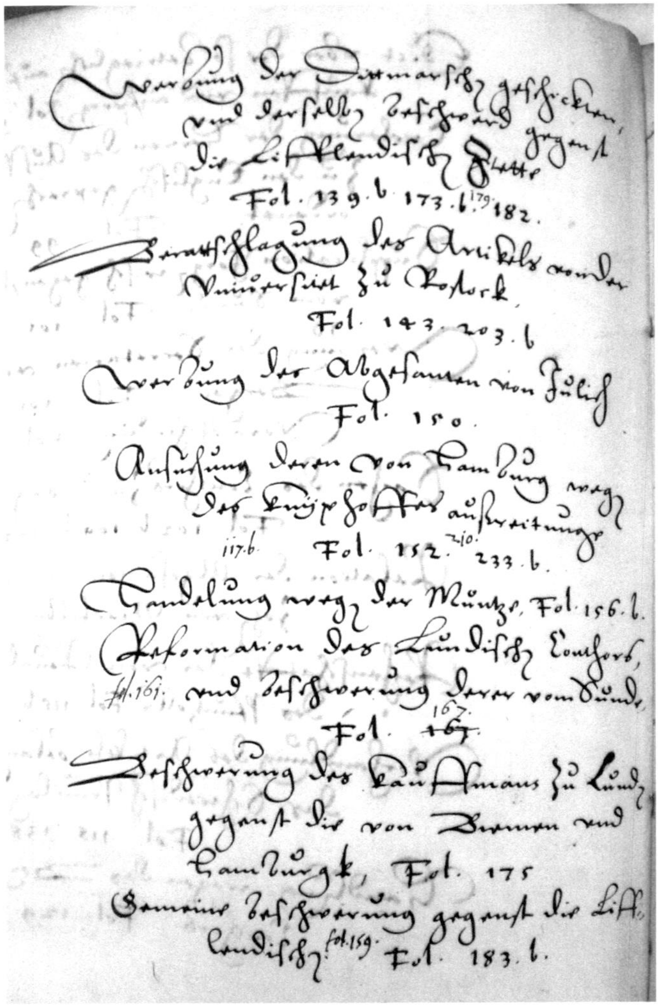

Figure 3.6d. Register at the end of the *Rezess* from 1540. Gdansk, Archiwum Państwowe w Gdańsku, 300, 28, no. 12, p. 4. Used with permission.

Even these large and heavy manuscripts were regarded as portable: after a diet, every town received its own copy, and delegates brought copies of older *Rezesse* to the next diets as points of reference. Some instances show, however, that towns also began to compile excerpts of the parts of the *Rezesse* that they deemed most important (see fig. 3.7a–b). The *Rezesse* were portable, but obviously at some point portability reached its limits: delegates could bring a copy of one or a few older *Rezesse*, but as the decades passed and more and more meetings took place, to bring all relevant *Rezesse* with them would have amounted to travelling with a library. At that point, delegates opted for preparing summaries and excerpts.

In sum, the Hanse documents show that a range of manuscripts could be portable, from small sheets of paper to thick volumes. Not surprisingly, there was a point when manuscripts were obviously regarded as too big to carry around, but the delegates found ways to deal with this problem by

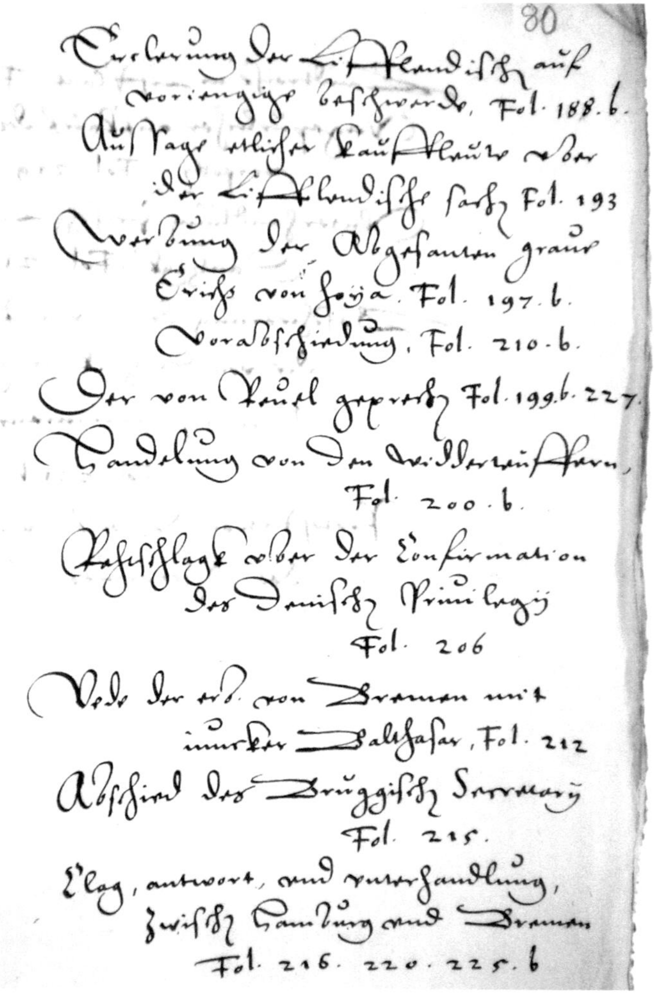

Figure 3.6e. Register at the end of the *Rezess* from 1540. Gdansk, Archiwum Państwowe w Gdańsku, 300, 28, no. 12, p. 5. Used with permission.

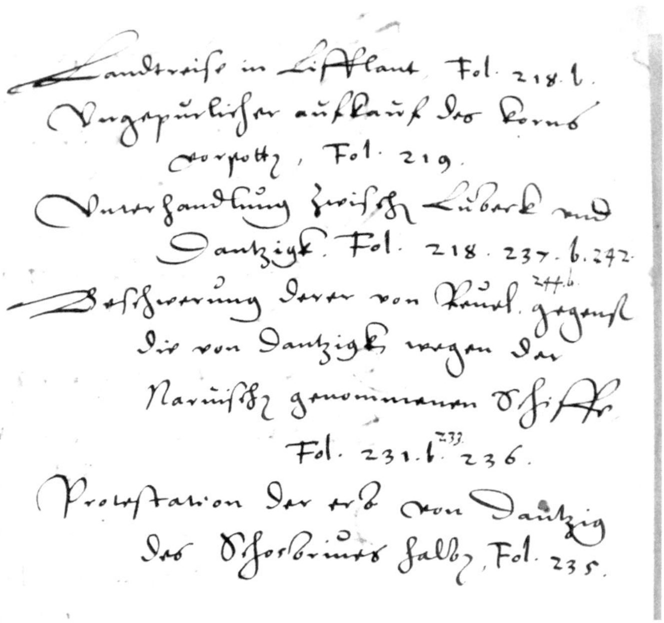

Figure 3.6f. Register at the end of the *Rezess* from 1540. Gdansk, Archiwum Państwowe w Gdańsku, 300, 28, no. 12, p. 6. Used with permission.

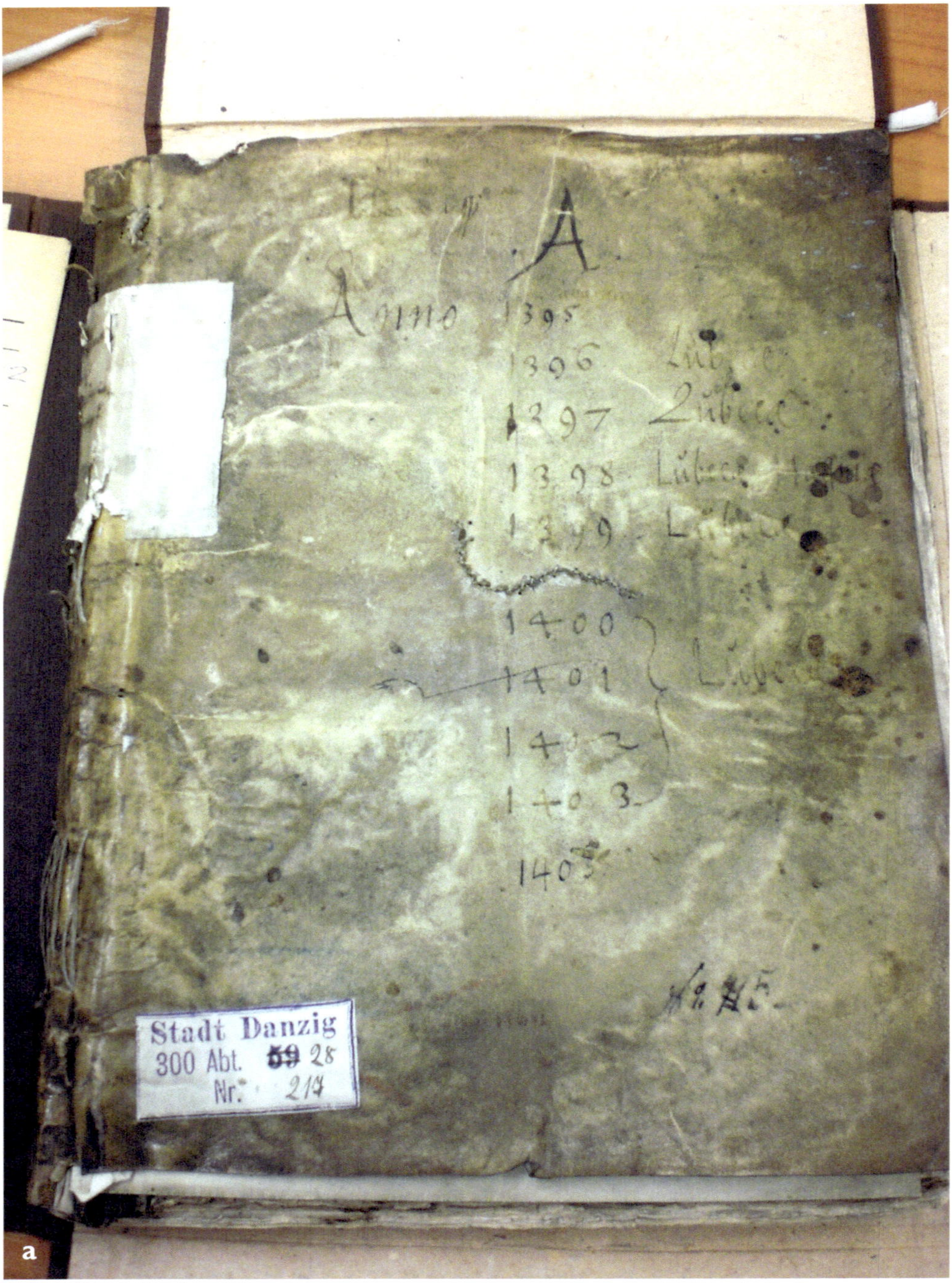

Figure 3.7a–b. Collection of excerpts of older *Rezesse*, cover and first page. Gdansk, Archiwum Państwowe w Gdańsku, 300, 28, no. 217, cover and p. 1. Used with permission.

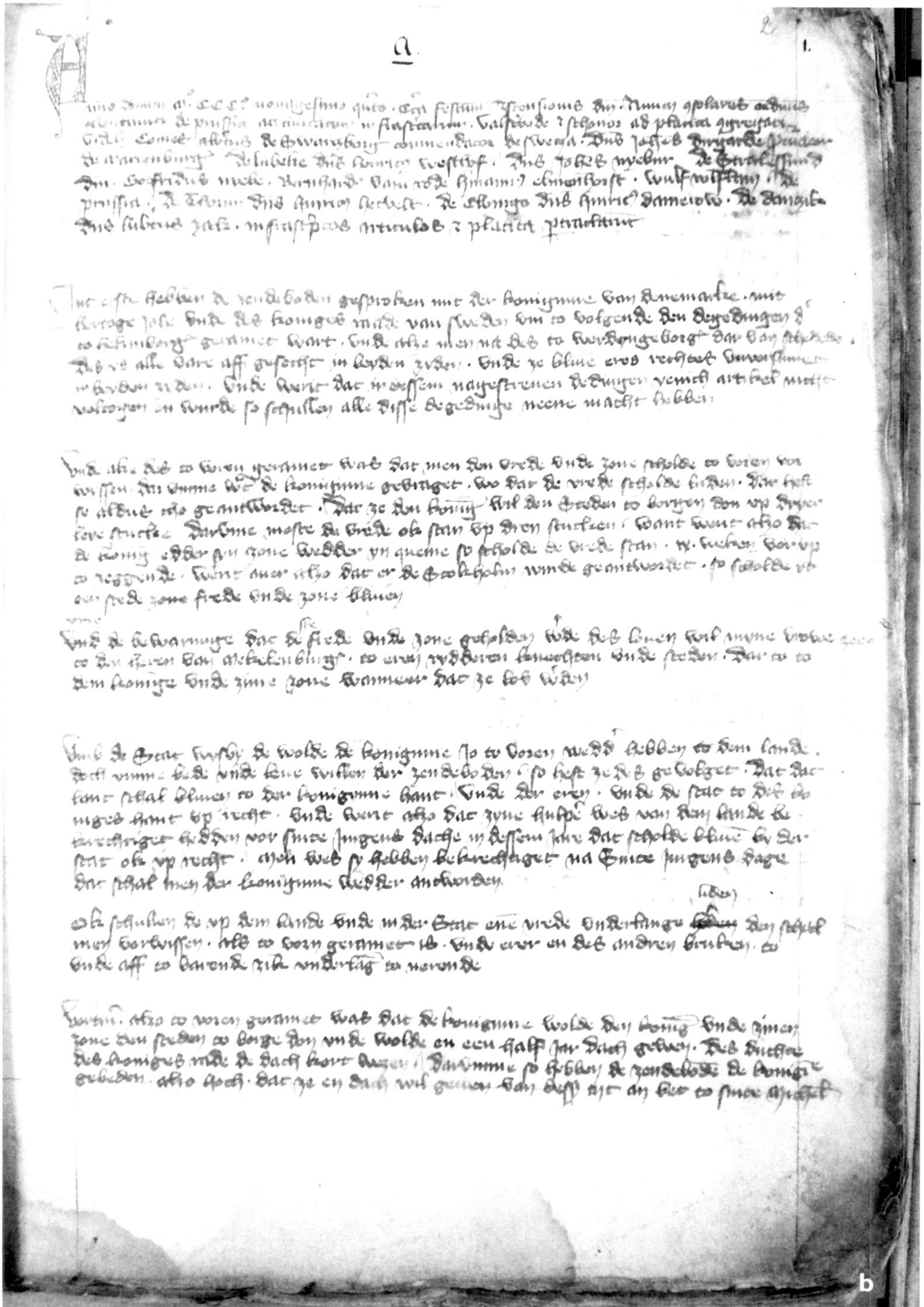
b

Figure 3.8a–d. Invitation to the Lübeck diet to Gdansk. Gdansk, Archiwum Państwowe w Gdańsku, 300, 28, no. 74 (1605), address page and pp. 1–3. Used with permission.

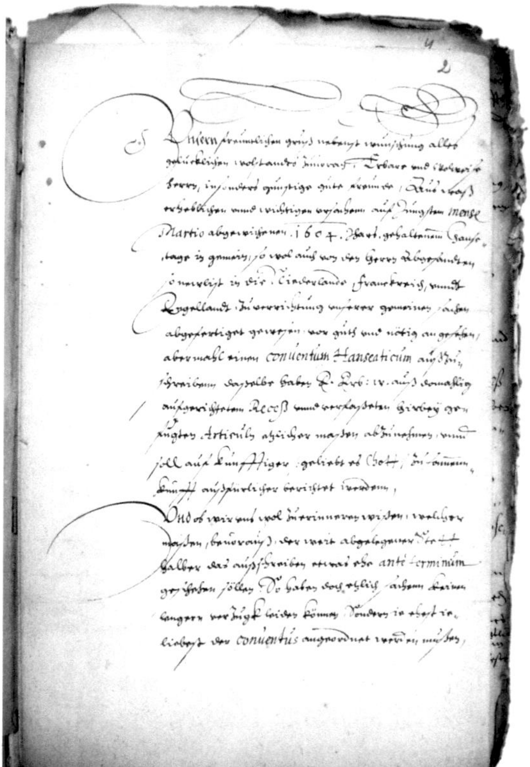

b

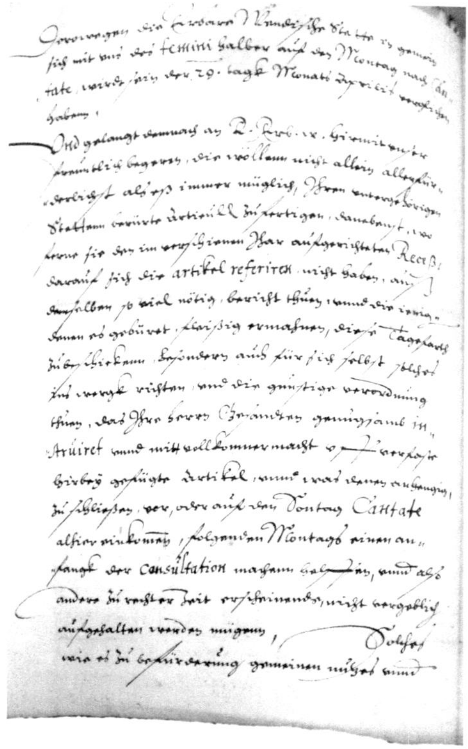

c

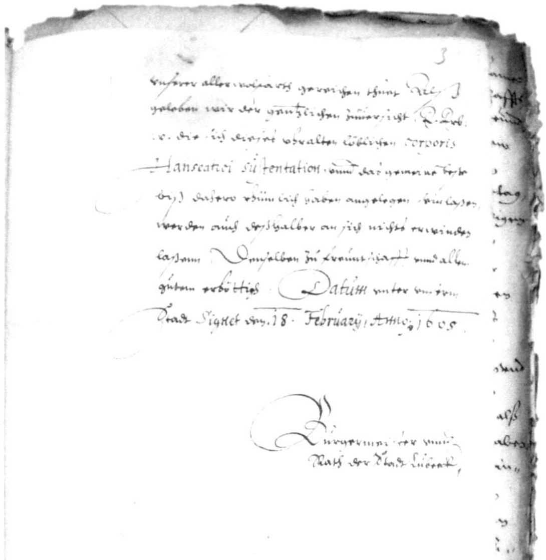

d

breaking down the large manuscripts into smaller excerpts. What is important here is that the portability of different types of documents served different functions, and this is analyzed in the remainder of the chapter.

Before the Diet

Communication between the towns started long before a Hanse diet commenced. A large number of towns participated in the preparations. As a first step, the town that organized the meeting sent out invitations (see fig. 3.8a–d).[22] In most cases, and also in the ones analyzed here, this was Lübeck. In 1518, the invitation letter was issued by "Lübeck and the Wendish towns,"[23] so obviously Lübeck had already involved the Wendish towns in the preparation of the diet.[24]

Lübeck did not send letters to all the Hanse towns itself, but rather asked the bigger towns to distribute the letter to the other towns in their region. In 1418, for instance, Lübeck asked Wismar to come to the Hanse diet and also to forward the invitation to Rostock.[25] During the fifteenth century, the towns increasingly understood their regional collaboration that had been going on for centuries as part of the large Hansecooperation. Initially at the *kontor* in Bruges, the merchants were grouped into three "Hanse thirds,"[26] and in 1494 the diet decided that the towns be classified into a Lübeck third (with Lübeck, obviously, as the head of the third), a Westphalian third (headed by Köln), and a Saxonian third (with Brunswick at the top).[27]

Köln answered the invitation to the diet in 1518 by declaring that they would come and also forward the invitation to the towns of its third.[28] On the same day the Köln chancellery wrote to Duisburg, Wesel, Emmerich,

---

22 Since not all the original documents survived from 1418 and 1518, the figures show images of the same classes of documents, but different years from the archive in Gdansk, where the documents survived in excellent condition.

23 The Wendish towns typically refer to Lübeck, Lüneburg, Stralsund, Rostock, Wismar, and Hamburg, though the letter does not state that the letter was sent by these six towns.

24 HR III, 7, no. 55.

25 HR I, 6, no. 555.

26 The statute of the Bruges *kontor* of 1347 states that the Hanse merchants are to be grouped into three parts, HR I, 1, no. 143, 74.

27 Dollinger, *Die Hanse*, 121–22. In the sixteenth century, Livonia-Prussia was added with Gdansk as a head, thereby turning the thirds into quarters.

28 HR III, 7, no. 72.

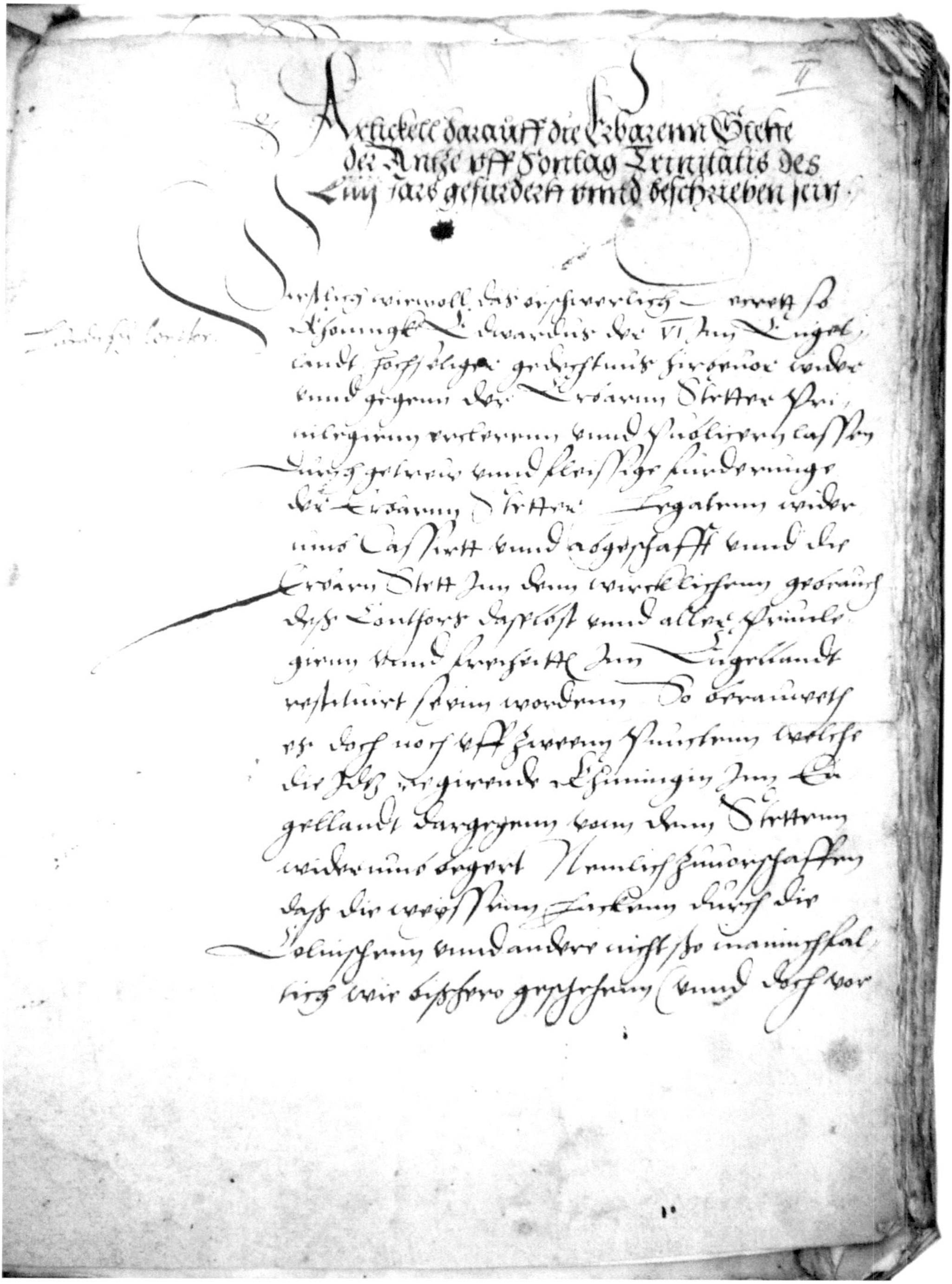

Figure 3.9. Agenda for the 1554 diet, first page. Gdansk, Archiwum Państwowe w Gdańsku, 300, 28, no. 24 (1554). Used with permission.

Deventer, Zwolle, Kampen, Groningen, Bolsward, Stavoren, Elburg, Harderwijk, Zutphen, Arnheim, Nijmegen, and Roermonde to pass on the invitation from Lübeck and the Wendish towns.[29] Köln also informed Venlo that it was not invited.[30] Venlo thus knew that a diet would take place, even if it was not being asked to join.

The invitation was hence not sent from the centre of Lübeck to all the Hanse towns. Rather, a number of towns participated in distributing the invitation. Alongside the invitations, Lübeck also sent out the agenda (fig. 3.9).[31] Every town was thus informed about the topics that would be discussed and could prepare its position on each of the issues. They could also make additions to the list, as the Saxon towns of Goslar, Hildesheim, Göttingen, Hannover, Einbeck, and Brunswick did in 1518. They sent Lübeck the topics they wanted to discuss,[32] and four weeks later Lübeck informed them that it had forwarded the agenda to the other towns.[33]

Not every town that was invited joined the diet in person. Town councillors who did not send a representative to the meeting, but still wanted to be considered part of the Hanse network, dispatched letters with apologies and excuses that were transported from the various Hanse towns to Lübeck. In 1418, Stavoren and Zierikzee sent their apologies to Lübeck stating that they could not attend because of unrest and war in Friesland and Holland, probably referring to the violent attempts of the dukes of Holland to conquer Friesland.[34] In 1518, Reval claimed that the invitation arrived so late that they were not able to plan and make the journey to Lübeck in time.[35] Deventer, Kampen, and Zutphen did not receive the safe conduct they wanted for their travels.[36] Soest also declared that it was not safe enough to go because of problems in their territories.[37] Königsberg in Prussia could not join because the Grand Master of the Teutonic Order did not give them permission to go. In his opinion the representatives of Königsberg had to take a seat that was

29 HR III, 7, no. 73 (12.03.1518).

30 HR III, 7, no. 74.

31 The picture is again from the archive in Gdansk. See HR III, 7, no. 56, for an edited version from 1518.

32 HR III, 7, no. 59.

33 HR III, 7, no. 63.

34 HR I, 6, nos. 569 and 570.

35 HR III, 7, no. 69.

36 HR III, 7, no. 89.

37 HR III, 7, no. 94.

not accurately reflecting their importance.[38] The letters did not give formalized clauses of excuses but rather explained the current situation of the respective town. These apologies as well as others by Reval and Dorpat,[39] Thorn and Elbing,[40] Osnabrück, Herford and Lemgo,[41] Paderborn,[42] Münster,[43] and Greifswald[44] were read aloud at the diet, as the *Rezess* states, the protocol of the meeting. The towns at the diet who heard these letters thus gained an impression of the current political situation in various parts of the Hanse area. This information could also be important for the economic dealings of their burghers. The sending of these letters presumably strengthened the sense of community between the towns.

Just as the invitations did not all come directly from Lübeck, the excuses were also not always addressed directly to Lübeck. Riga presented the apologies of Reval and Dorpat.[45] A number of towns from the Westphalian third dispatched their letters of apologies to Köln as the head of their third. Wesel, Emmerich, Nijmwegen, and Zwolle informed Köln that they would not travel to Lübeck.[46] Deventer, Kampen, and Zutphen sent one letter to Lübeck and one to Köln stating that they had wanted to come, but had not received safe conduct for their travel.[47] Arnheim, Osnabrück, and Münster did not only send their apologies to Köln, but asked the councillors of Köln to back up their excuses to Lübeck and the other Hanse towns.[48] Arnheim also appealed to Köln to represent them,[49] and Münster asked Köln to defend its interests, just as Münster had defended Köln's the year before in Lübeck.[50]

The intensity and frequency of letter writing cast a web of interconnections between the different towns, binding them together into a community. Even towns who did not attend were included via invitations and

38 HR III, 7, nos. 106 and 107.
39 HR III, 7, no. 108 §13.
40 HR III, 7, no. 108 §27.
41 HR III, 7, no. 108 §29.
42 HR III, 7, no. 108 §31.
43 HR III, 7, no. 108 §36.
44 HR III, 7, no. 108 §88.
45 HR III, 7, no. 108 §13.
46 HR III, 7, nos. 92, 95, 96, 98.
47 HR III, 7, nos. 89 and 100.
48 HR III, 7, nos. 97, 99, 101.
49 HR III, 7, no. 97.
50 HR III, 7, no. 101.

excuses. Furthermore, towns from the same region aimed at coordinating their positions and actions before the diet. The larger towns invited the others from the same region to meet for preparatory meetings. These meetings produced another bunch of documents that were transported between the towns, namely invitations to the meetings, excuses, and information letters about what had been discussed for the towns who couldn't join. In 1418, Riga dispatched the invitations to the Hanse diet to the other Livonian towns and invited them for a planning meeting.[51] The same happened in 1518.[52] Brunswick also called a meeting of the Saxon towns in 1518.[53]

In the western region of the Hanse area, three cities organized assemblies to discuss the impending Hanse diet. Soest forwarded the invitation to the diet to Lippstadt, Werl, and Arnsberg and tried to bring them together for a preparatory meeting.[54] Werl sent its apologies due to illness of their councillors, and we do not know if the others made it to Soest.[55] Two other preparatory meetings did take place, however. Deventer, Kampen, and Zwolle called the towns from Geldern, Kleve, and Overijssel for a meeting to discuss the proposed articles at Deventer[56] and then went on to organize another meeting, now including the Westphalian towns.[57] This assembly took place at Emmerich[58] without the participation of Köln[59] and ended with the decision of the towns not to send delegates to the Hanse diet in Lübeck.[60]

The towns of the western Hanse area thus did not participate in the diet—with the exception of Köln—but nevertheless spent quite some time debating the issues proposed by Lübeck and the Wendish towns. They were kept in the loop, so to speak, by the documents being sent around in connection with the Hanse diet and the preparatory meetings. For the towns who came to the Hanse diet, the pre-meetings enabled them to arrive at the

51 HR I, 6, no. 549.

52 HR III, 7, no. 67.

53 HR III, 7, no. 64.

54 HR III, 7, no. 84.

55 HR III, 7, no. 85.

56 HR III, 7, no. 79. They invited Nijmegen, Roermonde, Zutphen, Arnhem, Venlo, Wesel, and Emmerich.

57 See HR III, 7, no. 81 for the invitation to Soest.

58 HR III, 7, no. 87.

59 Köln sent its apologies, HR III, 7, no. 83.

60 HR III, 7, no. 90.

diet well-prepared and probably even with allies for the issues they deemed important.

Apart from the organization of regional assemblies, the towns also communicated with each other to clarify who else was planning to travel to the diet and if they could make the journey together. Sending delegates to a diet cost time and money. Maria Seier calculated that the delegates from Goslar to the diet at Lübeck in 1511 cost them 125 gulden, Gdansk even paid 1,220 mark rigisch to attend the diet.[61] It is not surprising that the towns pondered carefully whether they should make such an investment. Travelling to Lübeck seemed more fruitful if many other towns were present as well, since more colleagues could be met for informal talks.[62] Besides, more towns could better agree on rules for the whole Hanse trading area.

Brunswick hence let the other Saxon towns know that their envoys had already established that the towns from Prussia, Livonia, and Westphalia would come as well.[63] The latter ones decided one month later that they would not travel to Lübeck after all.[64] In 1418 the Grand Master informed Rostock, Stralsund, and Greifswald that he would attend the diet at Lübeck.[65]

The question of who travelled to Lübeck was also important for practical reasons: taking the journey together made it safer for everyone. It was easier to get a safe conduct together than for each town to apply for it separately. Soest hence asked Münster in 1518 if they planned to travel to Lübeck and if they had already managed to get the safe conduct.[66] Obviously they did not get a satisfying response because a few days later they wrote to Köln asking them about their travel plans.[67] Köln replied that they would go to Lübeck,[68] but this seems not to have been enough: two weeks later, Soest

61 See Seier, *Ehre auf Reisen*, 33–34. Seier calculates that in today's currency, these are roughly 28,000 € and 109,000 €, respectively.

62 Murray has argued for Bruges that the more merchants frequented the city, the more it made sense for others to trade in Bruges as well. He describes the emerging cluster of merchants as a network of multiple nodes in Murray, "Of Nodes and Networks," 2. The principle must have been the same at the diets: the more towns came, the more opportunities, the more reasons for others to travel to the diet as well.

63 HR III, 7, no. 64.

64 HR III, 7, no. 89.

65 HR I, 6, no. 554.

66 HR III, 7, no. 76.

67 HR III, 7, no. 78.

68 HR III, 7, no. 82.

again wrote to Münster and inquired about the safe conduct for the journey.[69] In 1418 Riga forwarded the invitation to Reval and asked as a postscript if the delegates from Reval could procure lodgings for the delegates of both towns if they happened to arrive earlier.[70] In 1518, Einbeck wrote to Hildesheim asking when their delegates would leave for Lübeck so they could come to Hildesheim to join them.[71] Köln planned to join the delegates from Geldern, Kleve, and Overijssel at Deventer to travel together.[72] They even set a date to start their journey (May 31) before the other towns decided not to dispatch delegates to the Hanse diet after all.

These travel plans had of course practical reasons, but they also intensified the net of communications between the towns. If the delegates managed to share the journey, this would give them the opportunity for informal talks about the issues that were about to be discussed at the diet. All in all, the ties between the towns of the same region prove to be an important part of the web of Hanse communications, and these ties could only be built by carrying larger number of letters from one town to the other.

During the Diet

During the diet, the circulation of documents helped the various towns to form one voice without sacrificing the position of individual towns. The town councils did their best to make sure that their opinion was heard and acknowledged at the Hanse diet. Their delegates did not have the right to negotiate with the others according to their personal ideas and convictions. They had to follow the instructions issued by their councils that they had brought along to the diet (fig. 3.3).[73] However, the delegates often frequented a number of diets over the years and typically counted among the more important members of their home council.[74] It stands to reason that these prominent figures negotiated with one another and maybe interpreted the instructions a bit differently than was originally intended. But this scope of

69 HR III, 7, no. 93. In the end, neither Soest nor Münster sent delegates to Lübeck, see no. 108 §36.

70 HR I, 6, no. 553.

71 HR III, 7, no. 63.

72 HR III, 7, nos. 77, 80, 86.

73 For the instructions of the Gdansk delegates in 1518, see III, 7, no. 111. The picture is from 1591.

74 Poeck, *Die Herren der Hanse*.

action did not amount to a free mandate. The delegates did not partake at the diets as individuals, but as members of their town council. They can be seen as the vehicle that ensured that the councils participated at the decision-making process at the diet.

Ernst Pitz has pointed out that the delegates of the Hanse towns can be regarded not so much as representing their hometown, as the delegates of French or English communities did at the proto-parliaments, but rather as embodying their community.[75] While in French or English parliaments delegates were perceived as representing their local communities, following the tradition of Roman law, Hanse delegates embodied their community. The delegates at the Hanse diets were thus characterized as having full power of attorney, but this did not mean that they brought a written procuration to the diet.[76] They had this full power in fact by being members of the city council, so they had to act in accordance with the will of their council at home. The delegates also sent lengthy reports to their home council, detailing the deliberations at the diet.[77] The town council on the other hand took care of their representatives for example by warning them about impeding dangers on their way back from Lübeck.[78]

The delegates were not accountable to the Hanse diets, but to their hometowns. The legitimacy of the Hanse diet was derived from the legitimacy of the town councils: the latter had a long tradition and were elected according to long-established principles, and the Hanse diet came into being as the place where representatives of the councils met out of their own free will.[79] The decisions and deliberations at the diet were legitimated as long as they represented the sovereign wills of the town councils. This was one of the reasons why the diets always took a clear stance against any insurrections in the Hanse towns. When any burghers overthrew their council, they were no longer allowed to participate at the Hanse diets.[80] The portable

75 Pitz, "Die Verfassung des hansischen Bundes in den Rezessen der Jahre 1435 bis 1460."

76 HR I, 6, nos. 556, 534. At the beginning of the protocol of the proceedings it is stated that the delegates had power of attorney from the councils; they are introduced as *vulmechtighe radessendeboten* (delegates with full power of attorney).

77 To Reval in 1418: HR I, 6, nos. 591, 592, 593; to Gdansk in 1518: HR III, 7, no. 113.

78 HR III, 7, no. 117 (Hildesheim to their delegates), no. 120 (Köln to their delegates).

79 Pitz, *Bürgereinung und Städteeinung.*

80 At the diet of 1418, the delegates underlined again that only towns with the traditional council firmly in place could be part of Hanse cooperation, see HR I, 6,

documents—letters, reports, instructions—established and fortified this connection between the diet and the town councils.

As long as this connection held, the diet could gain its own voice. This becomes clear from the documents that were carried to and from the diet and were either addressed to the assembled delegates as one community or issued by them. In 1418, King Henry of England dispatched a letter to the diet, addressing the delegates as a whole as the "honourable men, burgomasters and consuls of the maritime towns of the Teutonic Hanse of the Holy Roman Empire."[81] Other letters to the diet were sent by King Erich of Denmark,[82] Duke Heinrich of Schleswig,[83] Count Adolf of Schauenburg,[84] Count Heinrich of Holstein,[85] Duke Heinrich of Schleswig,[86] King Sigismund,[87] the Four Members of Flanders,[88] and the archbishop of Bremen.[89] The delegates at the diet also dispatched letters, speaking in the name of the community (fig. 3.1): the letters were not signed by the representatives of each town, but rather as "delegates of the common towns of the German Hanse etc."[90] To the king of England, they called themselves "the most obedient urban delegates of the German Hanse, assembled at Lübeck."[91] They sent letters to the Duke Heinrich of Schleswig and Count Heinrich of Holstein,[92] Count Adolf of Schauenburg,[93] the duke of Burgundy,[94] the Four Members

no. 556, §§60–62. In the years before, a revolt in Lübeck had posed considerable difficulties for the organization of Hanse activities.

81 HR I, 6, no. 581, "magne providencie viris, burgimastris et consulibus civitatum et villarum maritimarum hanze Theutonice sacri Romani imperii."

82 HR I, 6, no. 558.

83 HR I, 6, no. 561.

84 HR I, 6, no. 564.

85 HR I, 6, nos. 562 and 567.

86 HR I, 6, no. 568.

87 HR I, 6, no. 571.

88 HR I, 6, nos. 572 and 573.

89 HR I, 6, no. 587.

90 HR I, 6, nos. 580 (fig. 3.1) and 577: "Radessendeboden der gemenen stede van der Dudesschen henze etc."

91 HR III, 7, no. 114: "obsequentissimi oratores et nunctii civitatis anze Theutonice apud Lubecam congregate."

92 HR I, 6, no. 560.

93 HR I, 6, no. 565.

94 HR I, 6, no. 574.

of Flanders,[95] King Henry of England,[96] Duke John of Holland,[97] to the archbishop of Bremen,[98] and the Grand Master of the Teutonic Order.[99]

All these political figures and bodies thus interacted not with a collection of representatives from various towns, but with one community, the community of "Ratssendeboten" (delegates). These dispatches hence made it clear to rulers in various parts of Europe that the community of Hanse towns existed as an entity that could issue letters and be addressed as a collective.

This entity consisted of the towns, but was at the same time something different than just a coalition of various towns. The diet received letters even from towns whose representatives were present at the diet. In 1418, the town council of Hamburg wrote a letter to the diet which its own delegates were attending.[100] The Hamburg town council was thus on the one hand an organization addressing the diet and on the other hand part of the diet receiving the letter. The diet as a whole also addressed other Hanse towns that had sent delegates to the diet[101] or excused themselves (fig. 3.10a–b),[102] and the assembly received letters from Hanse towns that had not managed to come to the diet, but wanted to state their position.[103] The diet was addressed as a recipient when its session had not started yet, as in March 1418 by the king of England.[104]

The delegates also acted as a collective when hearing and answering the complaints by the *kontors*. The secretaries of the trading outposts at Bruges, Bergen, and London travelled to the diet and wrote letters with their complaints even when no diet was in session; they just sent their letters to Lübeck. These grievances were addressed, however, to the delegates of the towns as a whole, referring to them as the "delegates and councillors of the

---

95 HR I, 6, nos. 575 and 578.

96 HR I, 6, no. 582.

97 HR I, 6, no. 585.

98 HR I, 6, no. 589.

99 HR III, 7, no. 115.

100 HR I, 6, no. 588.

101 HR I, 6, no. 566.

102 HR III, 7, no. 116, to Bremen, Stade, Buxtehude, Thorn, Elbing, Dorpat, Reval, Osnabrück, Soest, Nijmwegen, Arnheim, Zutphen, Deventer, Kampen, Zwolle, Groningen, Harderwijk, Duisburg, Wesel, Emmerich, Greifswald, and Kolberg.

103 HR III, 7, no. 108 §390, letter from Dorpat about the common toll.

104 HR I, 6, no. 581.

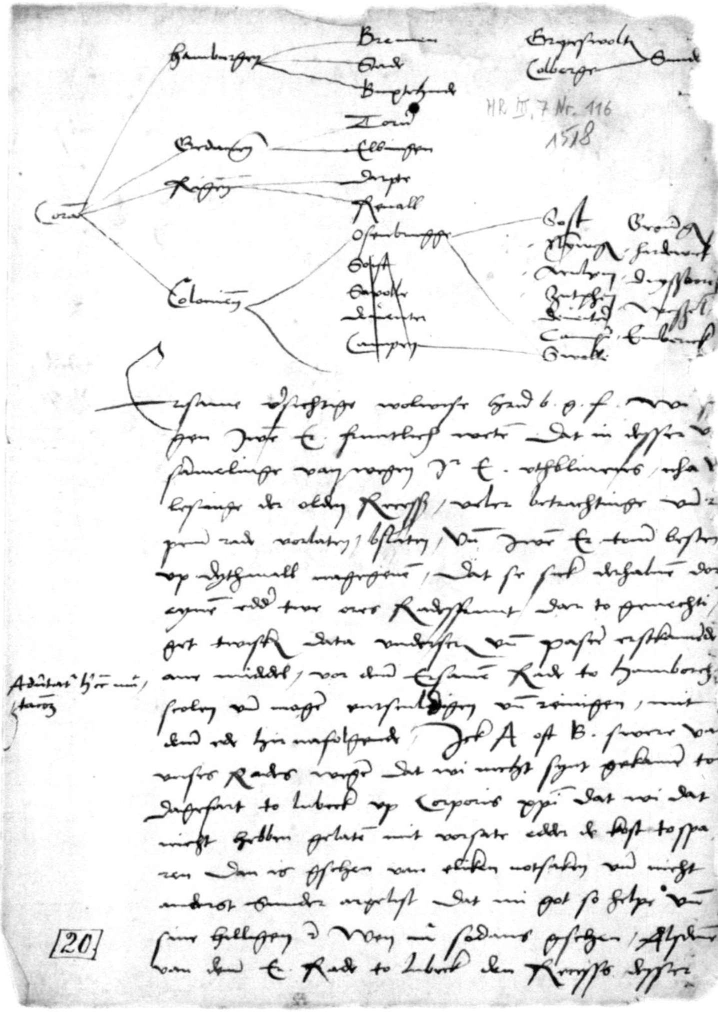

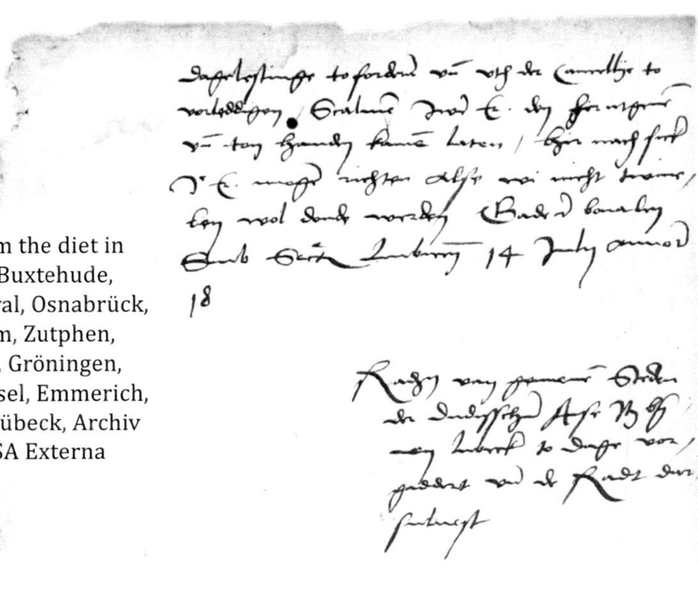

Figure 3.10a–b. Letter from the diet in Lübeck to Bremen, Stade, Buxtehude, Thorn, Elbing, Dorpat, Reval, Osnabrück, Soest, Nymwegen, Arnheim, Zutphen, Deventer, Kampen, Zwolle, Gröningen, Harderwijk, Duisburg, Wesel, Emmerich, Greifswald, and Kolberg. Lübeck, Archiv der Hansestadt Lübeck, ASA Externa Hanseatica 148a, pp. 1–2. Used with permission.

common towns of the Teutonic Hanse"[105] or "delegates of the common Hanse towns."[106] The diet responded to these complaints, thus speaking with one collective voice.[107]

The limits for allowing the diet to act as an entity were obviously reached when the representatives discussed whether a delegation sent to Antwerp should be equipped with a procuration of the diet as a whole.[108] Previous diets had also dispatched delegations, but these had been considered as delegations by the towns who had agreed to organize them.[109] Now the diet discussed whether to issue a procuration that would enable the delegates to act in everyone's name.[110] Gdansk, however, vetoed this decision.[111] Apparently Gdansk feared that with a procuration, the members of the delegation would act in the name of the diet, and not in the name of the town council they belonged to. It stands to reason that full powers to act for the diet would have endangered the participation of the town councils in the decisions.

The documents that were carried to and from the Hanse diet show the close interest that the town councils took in the diet. Their participation was strengthened by the communication between council and delegates, and the

105 HR I, 6, No. 606, from Bruges, address in full: "Honorabilibus et ingentis discrecionis viris, dominis nunciis consularibus communium civitatum hanse Teutunice proxime congregandis, et presertim proconsulibus ac consulibus covitatis Lubicensis, amicis nostris predilectis" (To the honourable and very prudent men, delegates, and councillors of the common towns of the Teutonic Hanse soon to be assembled, and especially to the proconsuls and consuls of the city of Lübeck, our beloved friends).

106 HR III, 7, no. 110, from London, in full: "Vor jw werdigen, wysen und vorsynnigen herren radessendebaden gemeyner hansze steden, itczundes hir bynnen Lubeke dagewysz vorgaddert" (To the worthy, wise, and prudent delegates of the common Hanse towns, currently assembled here in Lübeck).

107 HR I, 6, nos. 576 to Bruges and 579 to Bergen.

108 HR III, 7, no. 108 §381.

109 In 1487, for example, Köln, Kampen, and Deventer dispatched a delegation to Antwerp to talk about a possible relocation of the *kontor* there, HR III, 2, no. 204.

110 Since no Hanse seal existed, the procuration should have been sealed by the Wendish towns: "So hebben gemene heren radessendeboden densulven gantze vullekamen macht und bevel gegeven und belevet, dat men desulven vulmacht upt beste extendere und na gefalle under der ersamen van Luneborch oft Wendesschen stedere segele vorsegele" (The delegates of the towns have given and ordered their envoys full power and command to extend this full authority in the best manner and to affix the seal according to the decision of the honourable men of Lüneburg or the Wendish cities).

111 HR III, 7, no. 382.

legitimacy of the diet rested upon the legitimacy of the town councils who sent representatives to the diet. Once in Lübeck, the delegates participated in forming a collective entity that could issue and receive letters and even to a degree continued to exist when the diet was not in session. The legitimacy of the diet was strengthened because various kings and princes recognized it as a community speaking with one voice. However, the connection to the town councils had to be maintained.

After the Diet

After a diet ended, the minutes of the meeting were dispatched to all the towns that had been present, and to some others (fig. 3.4). If questions arose about what had been discussed at a diet, each town could refer to its own version of the *Rezesse*; they did not have to ask Lübeck for information. Each town thus formed a part of the collective archive of Hanse cooperation. The *Rezesse* contained all the decisions that had been taken at a meeting, and from the fifteenth century onward they also recounted the discussions leading up to the final round of votes. As mentioned above, the decisions were not immediately legally binding, but had to be transferred into local law, and quite often the only decision that could be reached was to postpone the discussions to the next diet.[112] Nonetheless, the *Rezesse* exerted a kind of normative force as the authoritative source for what had been discussed and agreed upon at a diet. Each town participated in creating this authoritative status because each town kept an exemplar of the *Rezess* and referred to its contents when it seemed useful.

Right after the meeting had concluded, the scribes of the host town (in our cases Lübeck) wrote out several exemplars of the *Rezess* and issued them to the participating towns.[113] The *Rezess* of 1418 survived in the archives of Lübeck, Wismar, Gdansk, and Köln.[114] The one from 1518 can still be found in the archives of Stralsund, Köln, Brunswick, Gdansk, Hildesheim, and Lübeck.[115] They cannot be regarded as copies of the Lübeck *Rezess* because all versions

---

112 The question whether to relocate the *kontor* from Bruges to Antwerp, for instance, was postponed for more than a hundred years from one diet to the next, see Kypta, "Von Brügge nach Antwerpen."

113 In the Gdansk archive, one exemplar of the *Rezess* 1577 survived that still has the destination *Dantzig* written on the cover, see Archiwum Państwowe w Gdańsku, 300, 28, No. 48.

114 These four served as the basis for the edition, HR I, 6, no. 556.

115 These six were consulted by the editors, HR III, 7, no. 108.

of the *Rezess* had the same status.[116] Only minor variations between the different exemplars can be determined. The possibility to issue an abbreviated version of the *Rezess* existed: the *kontor* in Bruges in 1418 received not the whole *Rezess*, but some extracts of the protocol.[117] However, the town councils usually received a full version of the *Rezess*. The *Rezesse* also contained all the letters that the diet as a community had sent and received since they were inserted into the protocol. Each town thus was informed about the proceedings at and the actions of the diet because the *Rezesse* were transported from Lübeck to the various Hanse towns.

Besides the *Rezesse*, letters concerning the distribution of the documents were also sent from one town to the other. Like the invitations, this communication about the results did not only go from a centre in Lübeck to the individual towns, but also connected the towns from the same region. In 1418, Lübeck sent the *Rezess* to Brunswick, and Brunswick ventured to inform the towns in its region that had not participated at the diet. They let Göttingen know that the *Rezess* had arrived, together with a table that should be posted in every Hanse town for everyone to see. Göttingen should send a member of their town council so that Brunswick could tell them what had been discussed in Lübeck.[118] Hildesheim requested a copy of the *Rezess* from Brunswick. If this was not possible, the Hildesheim council wrote, they would send a representative.[119] If this envoy would then write out the copy or if he would receive an oral report by the Brunswick councillors remains unclear, but obviously even towns that did not travel to Lübeck were informed about the proceedings at the diet. They participated in Hanse cooperation via the towns in their vicinity. During the fifteenth century, the diets developed formal rules for the representation of one town by another.[120]

116 See Kypta, "Creating, Confirming, Reconstructing Authority."

117 HR I, 7, no. 556.

118 HR I, 6, no. 603.

119 HR I, 6, no. 604: "So we juwe leve ghebeden hadden umme de scrifte, notelen unde articule, de ju de erbaren unse vrunde van den hansesteden overgehsant hebben, ifft dat wesen mochte, dat gi uns des wollen utscrifte ghesant hebben...mach des aver nicht wesen, dat gi uns de senden, so wille we de use dar umme gerne bi juwe leve senden" (As we had kindly asked you for the writings, notes, and articles that our honourable friends from the Hanse towns have sent to you, if possible could you send us a copy...if that is not possible for you to send them to us, we would gladly send one of our men to you).

120 Huang, "Die *stede van der dudeschen hense*."

In 1518, Lübeck tried to enforce some restriction in the dissemination of information, but apparently without much success. At the diet, the towns agreed that the *Rezess* should only be sent to cities who had submitted a valid excuse, and that the *Rezess* should only be requested from the chancellery of Lübeck and nowhere else.[121] However, a councillor from Soest informed his fellow councillors that an exemplar of the *Rezess* could be obtained either from Lübeck or from Dortmund. Since in Lübeck it cost four gulden, he advised them to get it from Dortmund.[122] We do not know if Dortmund obliged or told them to ask Lübeck, but the councillor from Soest obviously did not care much for the plans to centralize communication. The dissemination of the results of the diet hence brought the towns of a region into contact and ensured that towns who had not attended the diet were once again included in the circle of Hanse towns.

Since each town received its own exemplar of the *Rezess*, it could consult the protocol of what was discussed and decided at the diet without having to ask Lübeck for details. Each town built its own archival resources and could thus participate in remembering the decisions of former meetings. The contents of older *Rezesse* were frequently used as arguments during the debates at the next diets. The participants of the diet of 1418 scolded the Livonian towns that they disregarded the decisions taken at the diet of 1417, even though the Livonian towns had their own exemplar of the *Rezess*.[123] In

---

121 "[S]ick wo vorlaten to entschuldigen, und wen deme also gescheen, alsdenne elker stadt des begerende den recessz uth der cancellye to Lubeck und nergen anders to forderen gevende und totoschicken," HR III, 7, no. 108 §375. (They should excuse themselves beforehand, and when this has been done, then each town requesting the *Rezess* should seek it from the chancery in Lübeck and nowhere else, to provide and send it.)

122 "[U]nd so willen de schryvers dar veer gulden voer hebben. So late ick my duncken, juw ersamheyt konnen dat by den ersamen heren to Dortmunde so wol verlangen als hyr. Dar dan juwe ersamheyt des so nycht gesynnet is, kann ick hyr dat alle tyt wol krygen," HR III, 7, no. 119 (And the scribes want to be paid four gulden for it. So, it seems to me that your honour could request it just as easily from the honourable lords in Dortmund as here. However, if your honour is not inclined to do so, I can obtain it here at any time). His colleagues followed his advice, see HR III, 247n1.

123 "[U]nde dar gii ok grofliken mede gedan hebben tegen dat recesse in dem zomere nygest vorleden geramed, dar doch de juwen an unde over weren unde dar gii ok eyn recesse van hebben," HR I, 6, no. 520. (You have acted against the *Rezess* issued last summer, which concerned and involved your people, and of which you also have a copy.)

1518 the towns demanded an oath from the towns that did not attend the meeting, and they justified this by referring to the old *Rezesse*.[124]

The council of Gdansk used the old *Rezess* to prepare for the next diet. For instance, the Gdansk delegates got the instruction that they should protest that in the *Rezess* of the last meeting, the towns had deemed Gdansk's apology as not sufficient. Gdansk's reasons, they should argue, were as good as anyone else's.[125] We also know that in Gdansk excerpts of the *Rezesse* were prepared (see fig. 3.7a–b), presumably for the delegates to the next diets to carry them with them.[126]

The *Rezess* exerted a normative force because it was regarded as the authentic report of what had been decided at the diet. The delegates had to make sure that their position was accurately reflected. This can be gathered from the report the delegates of Gdansk sent back to their hometown: they underscore that they had made it clear that Gdansk could not agree to a procuration issued by the diet, and they had insisted that their position was noted in the *Rezess*.[127] The *Rezess* did in fact mention their objection.[128]

The portability of the different exemplars of the *Rezesse* hence ensured that each town participated in creating a kind of shared archive of the proceedings at the diets. This also enabled the town councils to use the *Rezesse* as argumentative aids and thus strengthen their normative force.

124 HR III, 7, no. 108 §145: "[D]at men darby faren schal na lude der olden recesse darup gemaket" (That one shall proceed according to the provisions the old *Rezess* made regarding it).

125 HR III, 7, no. 111 §4.

126 One such collection (fig. 3.7a–b) was already prepared at the beginning of the fifteenth century and holds extensive excerpts from the *Rezesse* of 1395, 1396, 1397, 1398, 1399, 1400, 1401, 1402, 1403, and 1405. See Archiwum Państwowe w Gdańsku, 300, 28, no. 217. Also, the whole *Rezess* of 1621 was copied in order to take the copy to the next diet; see Archiwum Państwowe w Gdańsku, 300, 28, no. 83. The document contains a note that the Gdansk envoy took a copy of the *Rezess* to a diet in Lübeck. See also Kypta, "Creating, Confirming, Reconstructing Authority."

127 HR III, 7, no. 113 §201: "daraf se ock protestereden und beden, dit also wo gesecht im recesse vorwaren tho laten" (to which they also protested and requested that this be kept as stated in the *Rezess*).

128 HR III, 7, no. 108, §382, 187.

Conclusion

The analysis of the two diets of 1418 and 1518 shows that Hanse cooperation rested upon an accessible flow and distribution of documents between the towns before, during, and after a meeting, which in turn was a function of the portable form of such documents. The same is to some degree true for every political assembly; however, it was especially crucial for Hanse cooperation because no hierarchy or formal structure existed to bind the towns together, and no authority could enforce laws and rules by power. The towns rather cooperated as long as they regarded the Hanse as a common project. Their participation hence had to be guaranteed every step of the way, otherwise the diets would have lost their legitimacy as the representation of the shared interest of the towns.

Before the diet, various towns participated in sending out invitations and organizing preparatory meetings. Even town councils who did not send representatives to the diet were informed about the agenda of the meeting, and sometimes they even offered suggestions how to supplement the order of business. By dispatching letters of excuses to the diet, the towns showed their interest in remaining a part of the cooperation, and by explaining their reasons let the other delegates participate in their troubles. The diet thus gained legitimacy because it was recognized by both those town councils with and without delegates at the diet—as an important forum to meet and discuss the current issues.

During the meeting, the representatives stayed in close contact with their home council via instructions and reports. The diet was designed as the assembly of delegates from numerous town councils, and the well-established legitimacy of these councils reflected on the diet. At the meeting, the delegates represented their home council and its interests, but they also forged a new collective, the community of all the delegates present at the diet. This community became manifest in the letters that the diet as a whole sent and received to and from various princes and kings in Europe. This collective was recognized as legitimately acting on behalf of the towns by these kings, princes, and also the town councils themselves who dispatched letters addressed to the community. As long as their individual interests maintained intact, then, the town councils allowed their legitimacy to reflect upon the diet and even allowed it to act as one collective.

After the meeting, the protocols of the deliberations and decisions were written out several times and distributed to the towns that had participated at the diet. A town that had not sent delegates could also request a copy or at least a report by a neighbouring town council. Each town thus participated in forming a sort of collective memory of the Hanse diets. If councillors of one town wanted to check what had been discussed at former meetings, they could consult their own exemplar. The legitimacy of the proceedings was strengthened because the town councils used the decisions of former diets as arguments.

All in all, the portable document helped to create, facilitate, and maintain a network of communications between the towns. Communication enabled the town councils to actively participate in the proceedings by shaping the agenda, forming alliances with other towns from the same region, by enabling a community of Hanse towns to emerge and act on an international scale, and by remembering this community and referring to it as an authoritative body. The participation of the towns in sum ensured that the Hanse diets were regarded as the legitimate representative assembly of the cooperation of merchant towns.

Bibliography

Manuscript and Archival Sources

Archiwum Państwowe w Gdańsku, 300, 28.

Printed Primary Sources

Danziger Inventar 1531–1591. Edited by P. Simson. Leipzig: Duncker & Humblot, 1913.

Hansisches Urkundenbuch. vol. 3: *(1343–1360)*. Edited by K. Höhlbaum. Halle: Buchhandlung des Waisenhauses, 1882–1886.

HR I, 1: *Hanserecesse. Series I: Die Recesse und andere Akten der Hansetage von 1256–1430*. vol 1. Edited by K. Koppmann. Leipzig: Duncker & Humblot, 1870.

HR I, 6: *Hanserecesse. Series I: Die Recesse und andere Akten der Hansetage von 1256–1430*. vol. 6. Edited by K. Koppmann. Leipzig: Duncker & Humblot, 1889.

HR I, 7: *Hanserecesse. Series I: Die Recesse und andere Akten der Hansetage von 1256–1430*. vol. 7. Edited by K. Koppmann. Leipzig: Duncker & Humblot, 1893.

HR III, 2: *Hanserecesse, Series III: Die Recesse und andere Akten der Hansetage von 1477–1530*. vol. 2. Edited by D. Schäfer. Leipzig: Duncker & Humblot, 1883.

HR III, 7: *Hanserecesse. Series III: Die Recesse und andere Akten der Hansetage von 1477–1530*. vol. 7. Edited by D. Schäfer. Leipzig: Duncker & Humblot, 1905.

Urkundenbuch der Stadt Lübeck. vol. 1. Edited by J. F. Böhmer and F. Techen. Lübeck: Asschenfeldt, 1843.

Secondary Works

Behrmann, Thomas. "Über Zeichen, Zeremoniell und Hansebegriff auf hansischen Tagfahrten." In *Die hansischen Tagfahrten zwischen Anspruch und Wirklichkeit*. Edited by Volker Henn, 109–24. Trier: Porta Alba, 2001.

Blockmans, Wim P. "A Typology of Representative Institutions in Late Medieval Europe." *Journal of Medieval History* 4 (1978): 189–215.

Dollinger, Philippe. *Die Hanse*. 5th ed. Stuttgart: Kröner, 1998.

Forschungsstelle für die Geschichte der Hanse und des Ostseeraums (FGHO). "Gemeinsam die Spätzeit der Hanse entdecken." Accessed June 30, 2025, https://fgho.eu/de/projekte/hanse-quellen-lesen.

Hammel-Kiesow, Rolf and Matthias Puhle. *Die Hanse*. Darmstadt: Primus, 2009.

Hansischer Geschichtsverein e. V. "Hanserecesse." Accessed June 30, 2025. https://www.hansischergeschichtsverein.de/hanserecesse.

Hardy, Duncan. *Associative Political Culture in the Holy Roman Empire: Upper Germany, 1346–1521*. Oxford: Oxford University Press, 2018.

——. "Tage (Courts, Councils and Diets): Political and Judicial Nodal Points in the Holy Roman Empire, c. 1300–1550." *German History* 36, no. 3 (September 2018): 381–400.

Henn, Volker. "Hansische Tagfahrten in der zweiten Hälfte des 14. Jahrhunderts." In *Die hansischen Tagfahrten zwischen Anspruch und Wirklichkeit*. Edited by Volker Henn, 1–21. Trier: Porta Alba, 2001.

Huang, Angela. "Die *stede van der dudeschen hense* und ihre Tagfahrten im 14. und frühen 15. Jh.: Entstehungszeit statt Höhepunkt." In *Kollektive Willensbildung in der Vormoderne: Hansetage im Vergleich*. Edited by Angela Huang and Christina Link, 111–46. Hansische Studien 31. Wismar: Callidus, 2024.

Huang, Angela, and Ulla Kypta. "Ein neues Haus auf altem Fundament: Neue Trends in der Hanseforschung und die Nutzbarkeit der Rezesseditionen." *Hansische Geschichtsblätter* 129 (2011): 139–55.

Jahnke, Carsten. "Die Reliquien jener grossartigen Bewegung: 'Die Recesse und andere Akten der Hansetage' sowie das 'Hansische Urkundenbuch.'" *Hansische Geschichtsblätter* 137 (2019): 1–42.

Jenks, Stuart. "A Capital Without a State: Lübeck *caput tocius hanze* (to 1474)." *Historical Research: The Bulletin of the Institute of Historical Research* 65, no. 157 (June 1992): 134–49.

——. "Transaktionskostentheorie und die mittelalterliche Hanse." *Hansische Geschichtsblätter* 123 (2005): 31–42.

——. "Zum hansischen Gästerecht." *Hansische Geschichtsblätter* 114 (1996): 3–60.

Kypta, Ulla. "Creating, Confirming, Reconstructing Authority: The Originators of the Hanserezesse," in "Originators: Transformation and Collaboration in the Production of Original Written Artefacts." Edited by Janine Droese et al. Special issue, *manuscript cultures* 21 (2023): 119–34.

——. "Von Brügge nach Antwerpen: Institutionen statt Organisationen." In *Hansischer Handel im Strukturwandel vom 15. zum 16. Jahrhundert*. Edited by Rolf Hammel-Kiesow and Stephan Selzer, 161–81. Trier: Porta Alba, 2016.

"Letterlocking: The Hidden History of the Letter." Accessed June 30, 2025. https://letterlocking.org.

Murray, James M. "Of Nodes and Networks: Bruges and the Infrastructure of Trade in Fourteenth-Century Europe." In *International Trade in the Low Countries (14th–16th Centuries): Merchants, Organisation, Infrastructure*. Edited by Peter Stabel, Bruno Blondé, and Anke Greve, 1–14. Leuven: Garant, 2000.

Pitz, Ernst. *Bürgereinung und Städteeinung: Studien zur Verfassungsgeschichte der Hansestädte und der deutschen Hanse*. Köln: Böhlau, 2001.

——. "Die Verfassung des hansischen Bundes in den Rezessen der Jahre 1435 bis 1460." In *Die hansischen Tagfahrten zwischen Anspruch und Wirklichkeit*. Edited by Volker Henn, 23–41. Trier: Porta Alba, 2001.

Poeck, Dietrich W. *Die Herren der Hanse: Delegierte und Netzwerke*. Frankfurt am Main: Lang, 2010.

Schubert, Ernst. "Novgorod, Brügge, Bergen und London: Die Kontore der Hanse." *Concilium medii aevi* 5 (2002): 1–50.

Seier, Maria. *Ehre auf Reisen: Die Hansetage an der Wende zum 16. Jahrhundert als Schauplatz für Rang und Ansehen der Hanse(städte)*. Frankfurt am Main: Lang, 2017.

Conclusion

PORTABLE MANUSCRIPTS CREATING NETWORKS OF COMMUNICATION AND CONTROL

JULIA BRUCH, KATHARINA HOFER, ULLA KYPTA, and PAUL SCHWEITZER-MARTIN

This volume is dedicated to an in-depth examination of a pivotal aspect of the materiality of manuscripts, namely portability. Portable manuscripts connected people and transported information over distances. Portability of objects in that sense had the function to create networks of people, enable communication, exchange information, and transfer knowledge between people, and thereby also exercise control over people. Taken together, the individual chapters seek to enhance our comprehension of premodern economic structures by concentrating on the crucial element of mobility. By means of a series of detailed case studies, all of which are centred around the mobility of manuscripts, these chapters provide a comprehensive picture of the way writing shaped the functioning of merchant societies within the Holy Roman Empire.

The case studies examine the purpose and meaning of portable manuscripts. The first case study focuses on merchants' books, emphasizing their portability and role in maintaining social and economic connections within fifteenth-century commercial networks. The examination of Hans Bruckner's merchant book from Görlitz demonstrates the manner in which these manuscripts facilitated trade during the medieval period. This is evidenced by the practical binding and non-linear bookkeeping system employed. The second case study examines the function of written documents within merchant networks, with a particular focus on the "Große Ravensburger Handelsgesellschaft." These portable documents, designated as *Rekordanzen* by the company, facilitated the dissemination of business and personal news among branches between the Iberian Peninsula and southern Germany, thereby contributing to the company's success. The third case study examines the role of document portability in the organization of the Hanse. The circulation of documents before, during, and after Hanse diets fostered political cooperation among northern German towns, creating a shared archive and a sense of community. The mobility of manuscripts is shown to have been crucial in shaping medieval networks, commerce, and governance across all chapters.

The case studies presented in this collection primarily focus on representative examples of manuscript usage in the late Middle Ages. Merchants' books were pervasive among those engaged in trade. While the documentation pertaining to the correspondence of trading companies within the Holy Roman Empire is scarce due to trends in transmission, it seems reasonable to posit that such communication was a common practice. The scarceness of extant documents from this era does not preclude the possibility that written communication was a pivotal element in the structuring of business enterprises and the sustenance of relationships. The Hanseatic League, a notable example of a merchant-led network, represents a distinctive case in terms of its organizational structure. The considerable number of cities that were part of this coalition, along with the major role these portable manuscripts played in shaping this community, make it a particularly noteworthy case. However, portability also played a role in organizing other governance structures where towns and rural communities cooperated, for instance in the Swiss confederation or the Rhenish League of Towns. The case studies presented in this volume are hence instances of a larger story: the mobility of manuscripts played a crucial role in making and shaping economic and political connections in the Holy Roman Empire.

Taken together, the case studies in this book reveal how portable documents created and strengthened connections between individuals, cities, and both political and economic governing bodies. They shaped and sustained networks because they facilitated interaction, communication, and control: on the one hand, the physical movement of documents enabled the establishment of communication networks that were integral to exchange, governance, and trade in the Holy Roman Empire. As manuscripts circulated, they carried information about debts and prices, the behaviour of business partners, which often were also family members, about natural disasters, conflicts, and about political developments. The written word became a conduit for the dissemination of information across vast distances, bridging the gaps between individuals separated by hundreds of miles or the span of several months of travel. Portable documents thus lowered information costs for merchants and rulers and enabled them to act more prudently. The portability of manuscripts thus constituted a pivotal element within the economic and political systems of the period. Merchants, in particular, were adept at navigating the intricacies of mobility, not merely in the context of goods and people, but also in the realm of knowledge. Their proficiency in navigating travel routes, coupled with their adeptness in utilizing written documents, enabled them to thrive in a profoundly interconnected European landscape.

On the other hand, the portability of manuscripts enabled various actors to exert influence and control. Whether it was a merchant's book or a legal charter, the mobility of these documents contributed to the establishment of tighter control mechanisms, as processes could be tracked, monitored, and regulated more efficiently across distances. This, in turn, allowed for the institutionalization of procedures, which laid the foundation for more structured and organized systems of governance and trade. The mobility of manuscripts facilitated tighter control over processes, which in turn led to their gradual institutionalization within broader political and economic frameworks.

These results of our analyses confirm a number of hypotheses that have been put forward in recent research, they shed new light on and bring together various topics of current discussions in different fields of research. First, the connection between the commercial revolution on the one hand and the increase in written documents in the commercial sector has already been well established. However, on the other hand, the expansion of trade is commonly regarded as the cause and not the consequence for the surge in writing. Our studies point out how a commercial writing culture emerged in connection with and in the framework of an increase in writing in other areas of life as most importantly in urban in princely administrations. Merchants often came into contact and had to deal with such official documents, so it stands to reason that the increase in commercial writing cannot only be regarded as a reaction of the merchants to deal with the expansion of trade. They also might have picked up writing as a practice used by their peers and superiors and incorporated it into their commercial practices. Writing hence was not only a result of trade expansion, but writing also made the Commercial Revolution possible by laying the ground for communicating over long distances. The portability of documents further enhanced the ability of documents to connect people across Europe.

Second, recent research has called for taking the materiality of written documents into account in many areas of research and also in economic history. By doing so, our studies could highlight the importance of portability of the manuscripts we analyzed. Their material features made it clear that they were designed to travel with or instead of the merchants. The portability of these documents obviously was of consideration during their production process, with particular formats selected to facilitate transportation. Smaller documents, such as letters, file folders or booklets, could be readily inserted into pockets and bags and transported with minimal inconvenience. Similarly, books created for merchants were designed with the intention of facilitating travel. In lieu of voluminous, unwieldy tomes secured with metal bosses and clasps, merchants exhibited a proclivity for diminutive volumes with flexible bindings. Such lightweight and flexible books could also be conveniently carried in a pocket or a bag, making them more suitable for the rigours of long journeys. Despite their diminutive dimensions, these volumes were crafted with considerable care, ensuring that they would remain secure and intact even when subjected to the rigours of travel. They were, therefore, an ideal repository of knowledge for merchants engaged in extended journeys.

Merchants generally possessed ancillary stationary books that remained at their place of business or residence, to which information could also be transferred; manuscripts also interacted with each other in this sense. These types of books are characterized by their size, scope, and hardback covers, often with bosses and claps; the physical design alone indicates that these books were not intended for portability. Larger codes of law utilized by organizations such as the Hanse were inherently less portable in their entirety. Instead, merchants or legal representatives would frequently create excerpts of important texts to bring with them, thus ensuring access to pertinent legal data without the inconvenience of transporting the complete volume of the minutes. In sum, the reason why manuscripts were made portable seems to have been convenience: portable manuscripts enabled the merchants to consult them at every point of their journeys, they helped the merchants to always have access to important information. By being portable, commercial manuscripts became a form of prosthesis to aid the merchant's successful daily conduct of business.

Third, our studies confirm that handwriting remained the common technique to create documents even after printing was invented. It is interesting to see that even the extensive record of the minutes of the Hanse diets which were copied several times were written by hand and not printed. Despite the advent and proliferation of the printing press, handwritten documents retained a central role in the organization of medieval societies. It would be erroneous to assume that handwriting was superseded; rather, it retained its significance, particularly in the context of personal and business correspondence, legal documentation, and merchant records. Thus, despite the introduction of print in the fifteenth century more manuscripts were produced in that century than the centuries before. The portability of these handwritten manuscripts enabled their dissemination across regions, facilitating communication between merchants, officials, and rulers. Since they were carried around, they could function as a source of reference even without being printed.

Fourth, the myth that premodern societies were somehow more static than modern ones has long been debunked as a myth, but the idea is hard to kill that somehow really dynamic developments only occurred when the printing press enabled a wider dissemination of writing and thus of new ideas. By examining the material and portable nature of various documents, we could again elucidate the dynamic character of premodern societies. The movement of manuscripts facilitated the maintenance of economic and social relationships across vast geographic areas, reflecting the interconnectedness of medieval Europe. The significance of writing in maintaining these networks is evident, as portable documents served as the conduit for exchange, communication, and control, facilitating the coordination of intricate activities such as trade, legal disputes, and political negotiations. Portability served not only to convey information but also to regulate the relationships between subjects, individuals of equal rank, and institutions. The portability of manuscripts facilitated the formation of informal networks that extended beyond the commercial sphere, encompassing rulers, politicians, citizens, and even other manuscripts.

Finally, studying portable documents shed light on decentralized governance structures. Historians of early modern political structures often tend to focus on the emergence of the modern state and regard this modern state as the outcome of processes of centralization. The chapters in this volume, however, approached the features of exchange, communication, and control in the Holy Roman Empire of the sixteenth century from a medieval perspective, so to say, not looking back from what was to come during the modern age, but studying how the dissemination of information, knowledge, and regulation were managed in a world where the modern was not yet known. The portability of manuscripts thus helps to see that governance does not necessarily rest on centralization.

In sum, the studies in this volume highlight how portability was essential for the dispersion of information, the governance of relationships, and the creation of networks that included merchants, cities, citizens, rulers, and subjects alike. Whether through merchants' books, letters exchanged between trading partners, or documents sent across the Hanseatic League manuscripts enabled the flow of information and power across vast distances. By focusing on the portability of these documents, we gain a deeper understanding of the premodern economic, social, and political landscape, where writing remained a vital tool for managing and sustaining complex economic, social, and political relationships. In conclusion, these case studies collectively demonstrate that the role of writing—particularly in the form of handwritten manuscripts—remained pivotal to the organization of medieval society, even in an era that was increasingly shaped by the printing press. By focusing on the aspect of mobility, this book provides a new perspective on the economic and social structures of the premodern world. They demonstrate how the movement of written materials helped shape the broader institutional and organizational frameworks of the Holy Roman Empire.

Printed in the United States
by Baker & Taylor Publisher Services